THE AQA A LEVEL POETRY ANTHOLOGY:

PRE-1900 LOVE POEMS –

THE STUDENT GUIDE

DAVID WHEELER

Red Axe Books

ISBN: 978-1911477068

© David Wheeler & Red Axe Books

Find us at:

www.dogstailbooks.co.uk

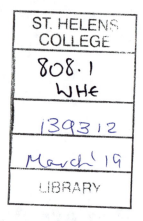

CONTENTS

A Level English Literature Assessment Objectives

AO1: Articulate informed, personal and creative responses to literary texts, using associated concepts and terminology, and coherent written expression.

AO2: Analyse ways in which meanings are shaped in literary texts.

AO3: Demonstrate understanding of the significance and influence of the contexts in which literary texts are written and received.

AO4: Explore connections across literary texts.

AO5: Explore literary texts informed by different interpretations.

Introduction

If you are coming to this book having read the Anthology, then I hope you realize that the cover illustration is intended to be ironic: very few of the poems (if any) treat the subject of love in the trite and clichéd way that the Valentine's Day balloons suggest. Richer, deeper and more complex emotions are at play in the poems in the Anthology.

I hope you find this revision guide useful. It consists of an individual analysis of each poem. The analysis of each poem follows the same pattern: there is a section on the poet and the context in which the poem was written and some facts about each author; unfamiliar words are explained; and then each poem has a commentary which focuses on both what the poem is about and the style, form and structure that the poet uses. A final section on each poem summarizes the poem's overall impact and effect. There are no colours, few illustrations, but you will get a clear sense of what each poem is about and each poem's overall effect.

I hope you will soon realize that the illustration on the front cover is intended primarily as ironic. Love – romantic, sexual love – is one of the deepest and most basic urges and an important part of what it means to be human, but many of the poems in the Anthology (and some of the exemplars I use in the introduction) deal with unhappy, unrequited love or situations which cannot be solved by a gaudy Valentine's Day balloon.

Who or what is this book for?

Perhaps you missed that crucial lesson on one particular poem that you find hard to understand? Good lessons are better than this book, because through different activities and through careful questioning and probing your teacher will help you to arrive at an understanding, an appreciation of the poem that you work out for yourself – and that process is invaluable – it's a process of thinking and exploring as a group, in a pair perhaps and as an individual, and, no matter how good the notes that your class-mates made, those notes are no substitute for having been there and gone through the process of the lesson. So, maybe, through absence, you feel a little out of touch with some of the poems: this book will help you.

Alternatively, you may want to read about ideas which you have not encountered in class. You may have the sort of teacher who allows you to respond in your own way to the poems; that is a completely valid and worthwhile approach, of course, but it does not suit every student: some students like to have clear guidelines about the meaning of what they read and to have various interpretations suggested to them so that they are at least aware of the overall gist of the poem. It still leaves you free to make up your own mind and have your own ideas, but it does provide a starting point – this book will give you that starting point.

You may be trying to revise the poems in the final days and weeks before the exam and want a quick refresher on poems that you first studied in class a long time ago; maybe it was a Friday afternoon and you weren't paying complete attention; maybe you were late for the lesson and never quite 'got' what the poem is about; maybe you were distracted by something more interesting happening outside and spent the lesson gazing out of the window. This book will help you get to grips with those poems.

It is very unlikely, but you may be reading these poems on your own for the very first time – this book will help you too, because I have assumed that you know nothing about the poem or about poetry, and the commentary on each poem is written so that you can start from scratch. Of course, some of you might find this a tiny bit condescending – and I apologize for that. I should also apologize if there are ideas in this book which are different from ones you have encountered before in class. There are as many different ways to read a poem as there are readers, and each reader might have a slightly different view of a particular poem – as we shall see. For example, most readers (pupils, teachers, professional critics) would agree that 'Sonnet 116' by William Shakespeare is about the nature of love – but how you define exactly what Shakespeare is saying about the nature of love is very much up to the individual reader.

So... if you want a book that tells you what each poem means; comments on features of style and structure; suggests the tone or the overall impact of each poem; gives you the necessary background knowledge to understand each poem – then this is it. At the end you will find a glossary of poetic terms and specific advice on how to answer exam questions, but after this introduction, there is a commentary on each poem – each commentary is self-contained and can be read on its own. Throughout the book I have used the words that I would use if I were teaching a lesson on these poems – if I use words you don't know or haven't heard, then look them up. Part of education, part of writing well about Literature is the way you yourself write, so to expand your vocabulary is a good thing. Terms which have specific literary meanings are all in the glossary at the back of the book. Indeed, Assessment Objective 1 in A Level English Literature states that you should be able to 'articulate informed, personal and creative responses to literary texts, using associated concepts and terminology, and coherent written expression'. You could make it a personal aim to learn a set number of new words each week.

Help Yourself!

I hope you find this book helpful in some ways, perhaps many ways. It deliberately includes information about the authors. An author's biography is an important part of the context of the poem. However, the internet is also a rich source of information about writers and their work – an internet search on any of your studied poets or poems will throw up all sorts of interesting resources, including student chat boards, online revision chat-rooms as well as more obvious sources of information like Wikipedia or web sites associated with a particular author. Where there is detailed biographical information here, it is because it is vital to an understanding of the poem.

But do be warned – all the information you can possibly find about a particular poet may help to clarify something you already sensed about the poem, but it is no substitute for engagement with the poem itself. And in the examination the examiner does <u>not</u> want to read a potted biography of the poet whose poem you have chosen to write about. Besides - generalizing from what we know about a writer or his/her era is a dangerous thing: for example, it is important to be aware of William Blake's political beliefs and to be aware that he wrote 'The Sick Rose' (discussed below) during the years of the French Revolution – some might say that without such an awareness the poem cannot be fully appreciated and understood – BUT that will not help you explain the impact of individual words and lines and images at all, nor will it help you write well in the examination.

Very often I have started my commentary on a poem with necessary information to help you understand it, but you don't need to reproduce all that information in the exam - it is there to help you fully understand significant details about the poem; to try to reproduce the process of discovery that a good lesson will guide you through. But it probably has little place in the examination.

You may be the sort of student who is doing English Literature because it is popular at your school. But it may also be that as you progress through the course you come to feel that English is a subject that you like and are good at; you may even be intrigued or fascinated by some of the poems in the Anthology. If that happens, then do not rely on this book. Look on the internet for resources that will further your interest. For example, if one poet makes a special impact on you – read some of their other work; you will find a lot of it available on-line. All of the poets in this Anthology sections are now out of copyright – their work is freely available on-line and at the end of some commentaries there is a suggestion for further reading. So there are many ways in which you can help yourself: it's a good habit to get into, especially if you start thinking about the possibility of doing English at university.

But please remember this is no substitute for a close engagement with the poems themselves. And just as importantly – this book is no substitute for a good lesson which allows you to think about the poem's language and ideas, and then slowly come to an understanding of it. After understanding it (and that is an emotional as much as a logical understanding of it), you may come to appreciate it. What does that mean? Well, as you go through the course and read more and more poems then you may find that you prefer some to others. The next step is to identify why you prefer some poems to others: in this there are no right answers, but there are answers which are clearer and better expressed than others. And preference must be based on reasons to do with the way the poem is written or its overall emotional impact: it's your job to put what you think and feel into words – I cannot help you do that. I can merely point out some of the important features and meanings of the poems. As you grow in confidence and perhaps read other writing on these poems or listening to your teacher or your classmates, then you will start to formulate your own opinions – stealing an idea from one person, a thought from somewhere else and combining all these different things into your own view of the poem. And that is appreciation. As soon as you say you prefer one poem to another you are engaging in a critical reaction to what you have read – in exactly the same way that people prefer one film to another or one song or performer to another.

The Literary Heritage

All the poems in the Anthology are part of the Literary Heritage and are generally by dead white Englishmen, although there is one poem by a women and one by a Scottish poet. That sounds dismissive (dead white Englishmen), but it's not meant to be. They are in the anthology to remind you that writers have been writing poetry in English for hundreds of years and that what happens over those centuries is that an agreement emerges about which poems are some of the greatest or most significant ever written in the English Language. How does such agreement emerge? Well, mainly through people continuing to read the poems, responding to them and enjoying them; another concrete way is for the poems to appear in anthologies – which ensures them an even wider audience. The point you need to grasp is that writing in English poetry has been going on for hundreds of years and what has been written in the past influences what is written now. Many contemporary poets will have read the poems that you will read in the Anthology. So when you read, for example, 'Sonnet 116' by William Shakespeare for the first time, you will be joining the millions of English-speaking people all over the world who have read and enjoyed that sonnet. Organizations like the BBC have also run public votes where members of the public can vote for their favourite poem – another way that we know which poems are popular. Such poems then become part of the canon. So part of our heritage, part of the culture of speaking English, whether you speak English in Delhi or London or Manchester or Lahore or Trinidad or Liverpool or Auckland or Toronto or Cape Town or Chicago, is centuries of English poetry and a continuing poetic culture which is rich and vibrant, and includes voices from all over the English-speaking world.

The Secret of Poetry

The secret of poetry, of course, is that there is no secret. Nonetheless, I have come across lots of students who find poetry challenging or off-putting or who don't like it for some reason. I find this attitude bizarre for all sorts of reasons. But some students are very wary of poetry or turned off by it. If you are – rest assured: you shouldn't be!

Poetry is all around us: in proverbial sayings, in popular music, in the nursery rhymes we listen to or sing as children, in playground skipping chants, even in the chanting heard at football matches. All these things use the basic elements of poetry: rhythm and rhyming and very often the techniques of poetry – alliteration, repetition, word play. Advertisements and newspaper headlines also use these techniques to make what they say memorable. Ordinary everyday speech is full of poetry: if you say that something is 'as cheap as chips' you are using alliteration and a simile; if you think someone is 'two sandwiches short of a picnic', if someone is 'a pain in the arse', then you are using metaphors – the only difference is that when poets use similes and metaphors they try to use ones that are fresh and original – and memorable, in the same way that a nursery rhyme or your favourite song lyrics are memorable. Even brand names or shop names use some of the techniques of poetry: if you have a Kwik Fit exhaust supplier in your town you should note the word-play (the mis-spelling of Kwik) and the assonance – the repetition of the 'i' sound. There must be several hundred ladies' hairdressers in the UK called 'Curl Up and Dye' – which is comic word-play. You may go to 'Fat Face' because you like what they sell, but I hope that when you go next time, you'll spare a thought for the alliteration and assonance in the shop's name.

Poets also play with words. So when students tell me they don't like poetry, I don't believe them – I feel they have simply not approached it in the right way. Or perhaps not seen the link between the poetry of everyday life and the poetry they have to study and analyze in English lessons.

Poetry has been around a very long time: the earliest surviving literature in Europe consists of poetry. As far as we can tell poetry existed even before writing, and so poems were passed down by word of mouth for centuries before anyone bothered to write them down. If something is going to be passed down and remembered in this way, then it has to be memorable. And, as we shall see, poets use various techniques and tricks and patterns to make what they write easy to remember or striking in some way - just as you may remember the words to your favourite song or to a nursery rhyme that was recited to you as a small child. Let us take one example. The opening sentence of Charles Dickens' novel *A Tale of Two Cities* is

It was the best of times; it was the worst of times.

It is not poetry, but it is very memorable, because Dickens uses simple repetition, parallelism and paradox to create a very memorable sentence. Parallelism because the two halves of the sentence are the same – except for one word; and paradox because the two words – best and worst – seem to contradict each other. Now look at this recent slogan from an advert for Jaguar cars:

Don't dream it. Drive it.

This uses the same techniques as Dickens: parallelism and paradox (or juxtaposition) and it also uses alliteration. It is all about manipulating words to give them greater impact – to make them memorable.

As I am sure I will repeat elsewhere, it is always vital to read a poem aloud: your teacher might do it very well, you might be lucky enough to hear one of the living poets in the anthology read their poems aloud or you can access many recordings via the internet. The AQA's own website has a recording of every poem in the Anthology. I think reading a poem aloud is a good way to revise it: it has been claimed that when we read something aloud we are reading twenty times slower than when we read with our eyes – and that slowness is vital, because it allows the sound of the poem, the turn of each phrase and the rhythm of each poem to stand out. As we shall see, the way a poem sounds is absolutely crucial to its impact – for one thing, it helps you pick out techniques such as alliteration and assonance.

One of the things we will discover is that poetry is partly about pattern – patterns of sounds, of words, of rhythm; patterns of lay-out too, so that a poem and the way it is set out on the page - often separated into separate stanzas (don't call them verses) – is vital. If you quickly glance at a page from the anthology, you would probably assume that what is on the page is a poem – because we have certain expectations of the way that poems look. So what? You have probably been aware for a long time that poets often organize what they write into stanzas. For me this is an absolutely crucial part of poetry because as human beings we are in love with patterns, we are addicted to patterns – and that is one of the many reasons we love poetry or find it so appealing. Patterns dominate our lives. We may have patterns on our clothes, our furnishings, our curtains, our carpets. But patterns rule our lives more completely than that: seen from above even a housing estate has patterns – the street lights at regular intervals, the garages and gardens in the same relationship to the houses; a spider's web on a frosty morning; the unique patterns of snowflakes; a honeycomb; your school uniform perhaps; the rhythm of your day, of the timetable you follow at school, of your week, of the seasons and of the year. And where patterns do not exist we like to invent them: the periodic table of elements (which you may be familiar with from Chemistry) does not exist as a table out there in nature – it's the human need to organize and give things a pattern which is responsible for the way it looks. Or look at a map of the world, criss-crossed by lines of longitude and latitude – and invented by the human mind as an aid for navigation.

What on earth has this to do with poetry? Well, poetry, especially from the past, likes to follow patterns and this structure that poets choose is something we instinctively like; it is also important when poets set up a pattern, only to break it to make whatever they are saying even more memorable because it breaks the pattern. We will see this happen in some of the poems in the anthology. Assessment Objective 3 at English Literature A Level requires you to 'analyse ways in which meanings are shaped by literary texts' – and they create meaning through words and simile and metaphor and the pattern that the poet chooses.

Let us look at it another way. Take the sonnet: if you choose to write a sonnet, you are committing yourself to trying to say what you want to say in 140 syllables, arranged in equal lines of 10 syllables each and fitted to a complex rhyming scheme. It is very hard to do, so why bother? Partly because it is a challenge – to force you to condense what you want to say into 140 syllables concentrates the mind and, more importantly, makes for language that can be very condensed and full of meaning. And, of course, the sonnet has been around for centuries so to choose to write one now means you are following (and hoping to bring something new and surprising) to a long-established form and tradition.

So what is poetry? *The Oxford Concise Dictionary of Literary Terms* defines it as:

Language sung, chanted, spoken, or written according to some pattern of recurrence that emphasizes the relationships between words on the basis of sound as well as sense: this pattern is almost always a rhythm or metre, which may be supplemented by rhyme or alliteration or both. All cultures have their poetry, using it for various purposes from sacred ritual to obscene insult, but it is generally employed in those utterances and writings that call for heightened intensity of emotion, dignity of expression, or subtlety of meditation. Poetry is valued for combining pleasures of sound with freshness of ideas....

Remember some of these phrases as you read this book or as you read the poems in the Anthology – which poems have intensity of emotion? Are there some which have a freshness of ideas? Or do some make you think about things more deeply (subtlety of meditation)? Perhaps there are poems which make you do all three? What can I possibly add to the Oxford Book of Literary Terms? Think of your favourite song – whatever type of music you listen to. The song's lyrics will share many of the characteristics of poetry, but the words will be enhanced by the music and the delivery of the vocalist. Is it a song that makes you happy or sad? Angry or mellow? Whatever it makes you feel, a song takes you on an emotional journey – and that is what poems do too, except they lack musical accompaniment. So think of a poem as being like a song – designed to make you feel a particular emotion and think particular thoughts; like some songs, the emotions, the thoughts may be quiet complex and hard to explain but the similarity is there. And that is another reason why it is important to hear the poems read aloud – they are designed to be listened to, not simply read. Short poems like the ones in the Anthology are often called lyric poems – and that is because hundreds of years ago they would have been accompanied by music. Before 1066 Anglo-Saxon bards telling even long narrative poems used to accompany themselves on a lyre – a primitive type of guitar and up to Elizabethan times lyric poems were set to music and performed. Even as late as the early 19th century poems by Byron and Burns were set to music and performed – including the ones in the Anthology.

Making Connections

As you can see from what is written above, a lot of the work in English on the Anthology is about making connections – the exam question will explicitly ask you to do this. Assessment Objective 4 at English Literature A Level explicitly asks you to 'explore connections across literary texts': the questions asked in the examination will explicitly require you do this, but it is a good habit to get into and the Anthology encourages you to do this: all the poems are about love – and love through the ages. You will find many contrasts too. As you study the Anthology or read this book you should try to make connections for yourself. Free your mind and make unusual connections. Certain types of poems (like sonnets) recur frequently in the Anthology; you might feel that some poems take you on a similar emotional journey; some poems might use metaphor or personification in similar ways; some poems were written at the same time as others and are connected by their context.

If you can connect poems because of their written style or something like structure or technique, then that will impress the examiner more than if you simply connect them by subject matter. Assessment Objective 2 requires you to 'analyse ways in which meanings are shaped by literary texts' – and this is where the commentaries below are invaluable.

Do you have a favourite word? If you do, you might like to think about why you like it so much. It may well have something to do with the meaning, but it might also have something to do with the sound. Of course, some words are clearly onomatopoeic like *smash*, *bang* and *crack*. But other words have sound qualities too which alter the way we react to them – and they are not obviously onomatopoeic. For example, the word *blister* sounds quite harsh because the letter *b* and the combination of *st* sound a little unpleasant; and, of course, we know what a *blister* is and it is not a pleasant thing. On the other hand, words like *fearful* or *gentle* or *lightly* have a lighter, more delicate sound because of the letters from which they are made. Words like *glitter* and *glisten* cannot be onomatopoeic: onomatopoeia is all about imitating the sound that something makes and *glitter* and *glisten* refer to visual phenomena, but the *gl* at the start and the *st* and *tt* in the middle of the words make them sound entirely appropriate, just right, don't they?

Think of it another way: just reflect on the number of swear words or derogatory terms in English which start with *b* or *p*: *bloody, bugger, bastard, plonker, pratt, prick, prawn* – the list goes on and on. The hard *c* sound in a word like *cackle* is also unpleasant to the ear. So what? Well, as you read poems try to be aware of this, because poets often choose light, gentle sounds to create a gentle atmosphere: listen to the sounds. Of course, the meaning of the word is the dominant element that we respond to, but listen to it as well. Listening to the sounds of poetry also means that you should get in the habit of reading poems aloud.

You don't need to know anything about the history of the English language to get a good grade at A Level. However, where our language comes from makes English unique. English was not spoken in the British Isles until about 450 CE when tribes from what is now Holland invaded as the Roman Empire gradually collapsed. The language these tribes spoke is now known as Old English – if you were to see some it would look very foreign to your eyes, but it is where our basic vocabulary comes from. A survey once picked out the hundred words that are most used in written English: ninety-nine of them had their roots in Old English; the other one was derived from French. The French the Normans spoke had developed from Latin and so when we look at English vocabulary – all the words that are in the dictionary – we can make a simple distinction between words that come from Old English and words that come from Latin – either directly from Latin or from Latin through French. [I am ignoring for the moment all the hundreds of thousands of words English has adopted from all the other languages in the world.]

So what? I hear you think. Well, just as the sounds of words have different qualities, so do the words derived from Old English and from Latin. Words that are Old English in origin are short, blunt and down-to-earth; words derived from Latin or from Latin through French are longer and sound more formal. Take a simple example: house, residence, domicile. *House* comes from Old English; *residence* from Latin through French and *domicile* direct from Latin. Of course, if you invited your friends round to your residence, they would probably think you were sounding rather fancy – but that is the whole point. We associate words of Latinate origin with formality and elegance and sometimes poets might use words conscious of the power and associations that they have. Where a poet has used largely Latinate vocabulary it creates a special effect and there are poems in the Anthology where I have pointed this feature out. Equally, the down to earth simplicity of words of English origin can be robust and strong.

Alliteration is a technique that is easy to recognize and is used by many poets and writers to foreground their work. It can exist, of course, in any language. However, it seems to have appealed to writers in English for many centuries. Before 1066 when the Normans invaded and introduced French customs and culture, poetry was widely written in a language we now call Old English, or Anglo Saxon. Old English poetry did not rhyme. How was it patterned then? Each line had roughly the same number of syllables, but what was more important was that each line had three or four words that alliterated. Alliterative poetry continued to be written in English until the 14th century and if you look at these phrases drawn from everyday English speech I think you can see that it has a power even today: busy as a bee, cool as a cucumber, good as gold, right as rain, cheap as chips, dead as a doornail, kith and kin, hearth and home, spick and span, hale and hearty. Alliteration can also be found in invented names. Shops: Coffee Corner, Sushi Station, Caribou Coffee, Circuit City. Fictional characters: Peter Pan, Severus Snape, Donald Duck, Mickey Mouse, Nicholas Nickleby, Humbert Humbert, King Kong, Peppa Pig. The titles of films and novels: *Pride and Prejudice, Sense and Sensibility, Debbie Does Dallas, House on Haunted Hill, Gilmour Girls, V for Vendetta, A Christmas Carol, As Good as it Gets, The Witches of Whitby, The Wolf of Wall Street.*

So what? Well, as you read the poems and see alliteration being used, I think it is helpful to bear in mind that alliteration is not some specialized poetic technique, but is part of the fabric of everyday English too and it is used in everyday English for the same reasons that it is used by poets – to make the words more memorable.

An Approach to Poetry

This next bit may only be relevant if you are studying the poems for the first time and it is an approach that I use in the classroom. It works well and helps students get their bearing when they first encounter a poem. These are the Five Ws. They are not my idea, but I use them in the classroom all the time. They are simply five questions which are a starting point, a way of getting into the poem and a method of approaching an understanding of it. With some poems some of the answers to the questions are more important than others; with some poems these questions and our answers to them will not get us very far at all – but it is where we will start. I will follow this model with each commentary. They are also a good way to approach the unseen poem. The five questions to ask of each poem you read are:

- Who?

- When?

- Where?

- What?

- Why?

WHO? Who is in the poem? Whose voice the poem uses? This is the first and most basic question. In many poems the poet speaks as themselves, but sometimes they are ventriloquists – they pretend to be someone else. So first of all we must identify the voice of the poem. We must ask ourselves to whom the poem is addressed. It isn't always right to say – the reader; some poems are addressed to a particular individual. And, of course, there may well be other people mentioned in the poem itself. Some poetry is quite cryptic, so who 'you' and 'they' are in a poem make a crucial difference to the way we interpret it. Why are poems 'cryptic'? Well, one reason is that they use language in a very compressed way – compressed perhaps because of the length of each line or the decision to use rhyme.

WHEN? When was the poem written and when is it set? This is where context is important. We know our context: we are reading the poem now, but when the poem was written and when the poem is set (not always the same, by any means) is crucial to the way we interpret it. The gender or background of the poet might be important, the society they were living in, the circumstances which led them to write the poem – all these things can be crucial to how we interpret the poem.

WHERE? Where is the poem set? Where do the events described in the poem take place? With some poems this question is irrelevant; with others it is absolutely vital – it all depends on the poem. In the Anthology you will find some poems which depend on some understanding of where they are set for them to work (clearly all the poems in the section called 'Place' are like this); you will find other poems where the location is not specified or is irrelevant or generalized – again it depends on the poem.

WHAT? This means what happens in a poem. Some poems describe a place; some describe a particular moment in time; some tell a story; some have a story buried beneath their surface; some make statements – some may do several or all of these things at once. They are all potentially different, but what happens is something very basic and should be grasped before you can move on to really appreciate a poem. Very often I have kept this section really short, because it is only when you start to look closely at language that you fully understand what is going on.

WHY? This is the hardest question of all and the one with a variety of possible answers, depending on your exact view of the poem in question. I like to think of it as asking ourselves 'Why did the poet write this poem?' Or 'what is the overall message or emotional impact of this poem?' To answer it with every poem, we need to look at all the other questions, the way the poet uses language and its effect on us, and try to put into words the tone of the voice of the poem and the poem's overall impact. Students in the classroom often seem puzzled by my asking them to discuss the poem's tone. But it boils down to this - if you were reading the poem out loud, what tone of voice would you use? What is the mood or atmosphere of the poem? Does the poet, or whoever the poet is pretending to be, have a particular attitude to what he or she is writing about? Answering these questions helps us discuss the tone of the poem. But you may not agree with everybody else about this and this is good: through disagreement and discussion, our understanding of what we read is sharpened. In the commentaries on each poem in this Anthology this question 'Why?' is answered at the very end of each commentary, because it is only after looking closely at the poet's use of language, form and structure that we can begin to answer it. If you feel you know the poem well enough, you might just use the section 'Why?' for each poem as a quick reminder of what its main message is. For all the poems the 'Why?' section consists of a series of bullet points which attempt to give you the words to express what the poem's main point is.

A Word of Warning

This book and the commentaries on individual poems that follow are full of words to do with literature – the technical devices such as metaphor, simile, oxymoron. These are the vocabulary to do with the craft of writing and it is important that you understand them and can use them with confidence. It is the same as using the word *osmosis* in Biology or *isosceles* in Maths. However, in the examination, it is absolutely pointless to pick out a technique unless you can say something vaguely intelligent about its effect – the effect is vital! The examiner will know when a poet is using alliteration and does not need you to point it out; the sort of writing about poetry that consists of picking out technical devices and saying nothing about their effect is worthless. I will suggest, in each commentary, what the effect might be, but we can generalize and say that all techniques with words are about making the poem memorable in some away – and this 'making something memorable' is also about foregrounding language. Language that is foregrounded means that is different from normal everyday language and that it draws attention to itself by being different – it would be like if we all went round every day and tried to use a metaphor and alliteration in everything that we said or if we tried speaking in rhyme all day – people would notice!

Warming Up

Before we look at any of the poems from the anthology, I want to briefly examine some poems to give you a taste of the approach that will be followed throughout the rest of the book. So we will start by looking at completely different poems. I am going to subject them to a full analysis, and I will demonstrate with the poems some crucial ways of reading poetry and give you some general guidance which will stand you in good stead when we deal with the poems in the anthology itself. This is not meant to confuse you, but to help. I cannot stress enough that these poems are not ones that you will be assessed on. They are my choice – and I would use the same method in the classroom – introducing a class very slowly to poetry and 'warming up' for the anthology by practising the sorts of reading skills which will help with any poem. Besides, you may find the method valuable in your preparation for answering on the unseen poem in the exam. The first two poems we will consider are both by

William Blake, so they represent good background material for 'The Garden of Love' – which is in the Anthology.

London

I wander thro' each charter'd street,
Near where the charter'd Thames does flow.
And mark in every face I meet
Marks of weakness, marks of woe.

In every cry of every Man,
In every Infants cry of fear,
In every voice: in every ban,
The mind-forg'd manacles I hear

How the Chimney-sweepers cry
Every blackning Church appalls,
And the hapless Soldiers sigh
Runs in blood down Palace walls

But most thro' midnight streets I hear
How the youthful Harlots curse
Blasts the new-born Infants tear
And blights with plagues the Marriage hearse

Context

William Blake (1757 – 1827) is now seen as the foremost artist and poet of his time, but his work was largely unknown during his lifetime. He was a painter as well as a poet and you can see some of his paintings in art galleries like Tate Britain in London or the Fitzwilliam Museum in Cambridge. 'London' comes from a collection called *Songs of Innocence and of Experience* which appeared together for the first time in 1794. *The Songs of Innocence* (which originally appeared on their own in 1789) are positive in tone and celebrate unspoilt nature, childhood and love. *The Songs of Experience* (from which 'London' comes) depict a corrupt society in which the prevailing mood is one of despair and in which children are exploited and love is corrupted.

This poem is often read as a profound criticism of the society Blake lived in. Everything in London is owned (*chartered*) - even the River Thames which is a natural force which one might expect to be free. Blake was writing at a time when Britain was the wealthiest country in the world because of its global empire and because of the Industrial Revolution which produced goods which were exported all over the world. But not everyone shared in this enormous wealth; the gap between rich and poor was huge, with the poor suffering really terrible living and working conditions. This poem first 'appeared' (this term will be explained below) in 1794. The date of publication is crucial: Blake is partly seeing London in this way because of events in France. In 1789 the French Revolution began, changing French society forever and ushering in a new age of freedom, equality and brotherhood. Many English people saw what was happening in France and thought it was good to have a society based on greater equality; they looked critically at British society and saw appalling inequalities and injustices. For example, you may be aware that this was the period in British history that some people campaigned against slavery in the British Empire: what is less well-known is that forms of slavery existed in London. There are recorded cases of parents selling their sons to master chimneysweeps in London. The life of a chimney sweep was likely to be short: they were sent up the chimneys of large houses to clean them. Some suffocated; others were trapped in the confined space and died; sometimes their masters would light fires below them to encourage them to work faster – they sometimes were burnt alive. For those who survived, their health was affected: they suffered from terrible lung complaints as a result of breathing in coal dust and, because of poor hygiene, might also succumb to testicular cancer brought on by the accumulated layers of biting coal dust.

Blake had produced *Songs of Innocence* on its own in 1789, although we can tell from his surviving notebooks that he always intended to write *Songs of Experience*. I have used the term 'appeared' because they were not published in a conventional sense. Blake produced each copy of *Songs of Innocence and of Experience* at home by hand and copies were then given to friends and acquaintances. Part of this was Blake's own choice, but we can easily see that his views about Britain and its government would have been highly controversial, so open publication of them may have led to charges of sedition or treason. The British government at the time were terrified of a revolution here, like the one in France, and were doing everything they could to silence people like Blake who were critical of the society in which they lived.

The paragraph above is important because it tells us about the context in which Blake wrote. Assessment Objective 3 at English Literature A level requires you to 'demonstrate understanding of the significance and influence of the contexts in which literary texts are written and received'. A key word in that objective is 'contexts' in the plural, because there are many contexts to any work of literature – the biographical, the social, the historic, the religious, the literary – and even our own context reading the poems now in the 21st century.

Blake earned his living as an engraver. Before photographs and modern ways of reproducing images, engravings were the cheapest and easiest way of illustrating a book. Blake produced illustrations for other people's books throughout his life – that was how he earned a living. To create an engraving, the engraver has to carve, with a specialist knife, lines on a metal plate; when the plate is then covered in ink and pressed on paper the lines appear on the paper.

On page 24 you can see (in black and white) Blake's illustration for 'London'. The overall impression is of darkness, which is appropriate given the poem. However, a shaft of light illuminates a young boy who is apparently leading an old and infirm man using a crutch to walk. It comes across as an example of kindness and empathy which works against the gloom of the poem and perhaps can therefore be seen as a symbol of hope.

Blake used the same technique for reproducing his own poems. After coating the metal plate with ink and producing the outline, Blake coloured each page of each copy of *Songs of Innocence and of Experience* by hand with water colour paint. It is estimated that only 25 copies were produced in his lifetime. If you go to the British Museum you can see one copy: it is tiny and exquisitely detailed and, of course, very personal, because Blake coloured it by hand himself. In addition, to produce his poems in this way was time-consuming and arduous, since in order for the words to appear the right way round when the page was printed, they had to be written in mirror hand-writing on the plate – a painstaking process that must have taken hours and shows not only Blake's artistry, but also his devotion to hard work.

Charter'd – owned. A charter was a legal document proving possession.

mark – to notice.

marks – signs.

ban – a government edict banning people from doing something.

manacles – handcuffs or leg-irons.

hapless – unlucky.

harlot – prostitute.

marriage hearse – an oxymoron; Blake juxtaposes the idea of death (hearses carry the dead body to the graveyard) with life – marriage often produces children.

Who? The narrator recounts what he sees in the first stanza and in the next three stanzas what he hears as he wanders around London. The poem is written in the present tense which gives it an immediacy and greater impact.

When? 1794.

Where? London.

What? The narrator sees and hears a population suffering and full of pain and despair.

Commentary

The poem's narrator wanders through the streets of London looking at the suffering of his fellow citizens which is apparent on their faces. The first stanza concentrates on what he sees; the second stanza changes to the sounds he can hear and this continues until the end of the poem. Everywhere he goes he sees people who are repressed and downtrodden; in the third stanza he hears the cry of a chimney sweep and the sigh of a soldier; in the final stanza, at night, at midnight, he hears the curse of *the youthful harlot* (very young prostitute) whose *curse* rings out in the night and *blasts* the *marriage-hearse*. We might note that there is no interaction between Blake and the sights and sounds he sees; the only interaction that there is evidence of is the *new-born infant* in the final stanza – the product of a sexual act – but the baby cries and is born into a world of misery and degradation. Nowhere in the poem do we meet a complete human being: we see their marks and hear them, but there is no encounter with any complete human being, suggesting at once their isolation, but also their lack of completeness and community in this horrifying city.

In the first stanza Blake uses simple repetition of the word *chartered* and *marks* (although with a slightly different meaning). The oppression he sees is all-consuming – he sees it in every face he meets. Note the last line which uses parallelism of sound:

Marks of weakness, marks of woe.

The word *mark* is repeated and is then followed by two words which alliterate. This combination of the letter *m* and *w* is very soft and gentle and creates a sense of overwhelming sadness. Note how *mark* starts as a verb in a very innocuous sense and then becomes a repeated noun, suggesting that there is an indelible mark on all the citizens of London.

The second stanza picks up the word *every* and repeats it five times to suggest the situation he is describing is all–encompassing. Again the final line is significant. The manacles that imprison people are *mind-forged* – they are forged, made in the mind. Is Blake suggesting that the people of London are not even aware of their own oppression? Is it something in their mentality, their minds, which prevents them from protesting? Do they have too much faith in their own rulers? Do they not question the system? Note too how Blake delays the verb of the second stanza – *I hear* – until the very last two words of the stanza. Blake's use of repetition in the first two stanzas has another purpose: his language becomes as restricted and limited as the lives of the people he describes. The word *ban* often stirs some debate: you may read elsewhere that it is a reference to the marriage banns – the announcements of a couple's intention to marry. This ties in with the final stanza, but, according to the Oxford English Dictionary, marriage banns have never been spelt with a single *n*. Isn't it more likely that Blake means prohibitions, banning something? Such as public meetings to protest about the condition of the country?

The third stanza continues with the sounds of London: the cry of the chimney sweep and the sigh of the soldier. Why is the church *black'ning*? Some readers suggest that it is a result of pollution caused by industry, but it could be a comment on the moral corruption of the church – it is evil. Why? I think Blake would suggest it is hypocritical: it is appalled by the cry of the chimney sweep, but does nothing to stop slavery and parents selling their children. The Church preaches a message of love, but does nothing practical to help the poor. The sibilance in lines 11 and 12 suggest the agony of the soldier. It is an astonishing image – sighs do not run in blood. But the soldier is badly wounded or dying – and he seems to be defending the palace or is at least in the pay of the place where the royal family live. Blake uses synecdoche to great effect in this stanza with his use of the words *church* and *palace*: its use here is partly to protect Blake in the repressive society he lived in, but it also serves to distance the establishment and the royal family even further from their subjects.

The worst horrors are saved until the fourth stanza and Blake signals this by stating – *but most* – and what he hears most of all is the curse of the youthful harlot. You can sometimes read that this is a curse in the sense of a bad spell, but it might just as well be a shouted swear word (*curse* had that meaning too). Who she is cursing is unclear, but the curse *blasts the new-born infant's tear*. Perhaps this is an unwanted baby, another mouth to feed, its father one of her clients? The baby is crying and in the final cryptic, oxymoronic line, her curse

blights with plagues the marriage hearse.

The phrase *marriage hearse* is an oxymoron because we normally associate marriage with new life and happiness, whereas we associate hearses with funerals and sadness, so to put the two ideas together is striking and original. Does Blake mean that some marriages are like death? Or that marriage is the death of love? Is marriage something that the youthful harlot will never know? Or is it the marriage of one of her clients? Why do married men visit prostitutes? Some readers even suggest that the curse of the harlot is some sort of sexually transmitted disease which the harlot has given to her client who has then passed it on to his wife – this reading might be supported by the word *plagues*. But *plagues* can be a metaphor too – whatever interpretation you choose, it is wise not to be too dogmatic – the beauty and brilliance of Blake is that he is able to suggest all the above possibilities – and even more.

What is certain is that there is something very wrong with marriage in this final stanza and that the curse of the harlot is frightening and chilling: note Blake's use of harsh plosive consonants in *blasts, blights and plagues* – this is almost onomatopoeic in its presentation of a diseased, corrupt society and Blake's angry reaction to it. We have already mentioned the oxymoron with which the poem ends, but Blake in the third stanza had already juxtaposed things which are not normally associated with each other: the cry of the chimney sweep with the church, and the sigh of the soldier with the palace walls – both these images in a way are oxymoronic. Think back to our comments on 'The Sick Rose' in the introduction – this is a profound and moving criticism of Blake's society.

Finally, Blake's use of the ballad form is important. The ballad form is associated with the oral tradition and with anonymity – it is a more democratic form than the sonnet. However, traditional ballads have a strong narrative drive which this poem lacks. So we can say that Blake takes a form that is popular and egalitarian, and then turns its narrative conventions upside down by writing a poem that is descriptive and very subversive and thought-provoking.

The Final Unpublished Stanza

This is the stanza that was found in Blake's notebooks when he died and which some editions of his complete works publish. As you read it, think about why Blake did not publish this stanza during his lifetime:

Remove away that blackening church;

Remove away that marriage hearse;

Remove away that man of blood –

You'll quite remove the ancient curse!

This makes explicit what is implied in the poem: Blake is calling for a revolution which will *remove* the church and the monarchy: *man of blood* is a phrase famously used by Oliver Cromwell to describe Charles I, the English king who was executed after losing the English Civil War. One can only guess why Blake did not include this stanza, but we can speculate that in 1794 it was too dangerous and that Blake might have got in trouble with the authorities for publishing such a call. Artistically the stanza has its limitations: *remove away* is tautological and, because it makes completely clear Blake's attitude to the things described in the poem as we read it today, one can argue that takes away the cryptic, mysterious quality of Blake's poem as it first appeared. This cryptic nature of the poem encourages us to think and analyze what Blake is saying and thus we are encouraged by the poem to break out of our own *mind-forged manacles*, to expand our minds in order to realize the full impact, the complete implications of what Blake's view of London is. London needs to be changed urgently and by a revolution.

Conflict and Power

The clear holders of power in this poem are the monarchy, the Church and the State. They use their power to oppress the population of London. There are clear hints of conflict in the poem – the chimney sweeper's cry, the soldier's sigh, the curse of the harlot – but the inhabitants of London are rendered essentially powerless by their "mind-forged manacles". They suffer from what Karl Marx was to call "false consciousness" – they are oppressed but are unaware of their oppression. In a sense, there is conflict between the poet and his fellow citizens: he sees their "marks of weakness", he hears the sounds of sadness and suffering, but he does so alone. His fellow citizens are trapped in their "mind-forged manacles". The final unpublished stanza, with its unambiguous call to revolution, indicates the power that the masses have – if they choose to use it.

Romanticism

In this cluster of poems some are designated Romantic poems and it is important that you have an understanding of what Romanticism was. It has very little to do with the word 'romantic' as we apply it today to an event like Valentine's Day.

Romanticism is the name given to the artistic, political and cultural movement that emerged in England and Germany in the 1790s and in the rest of Europe in the 1820s and beyond. It was a movement that saw great changes in literature, painting, sculpture, architecture and music, and found its catalyst in the new philosophical ideas of Jean Jacques Rousseau and Thomas Paine, and in response to the American, French and Industrial Revolutions. Its chief emphasis was on freedom of individual self-expression, sincerity, spontaneity and originality, but it also looked to the distant past of the Middle Ages for some of its inspiration. In Romantic thought the nature of the poet changed: no longer was a poet someone who could manipulate words well and with skill; the poet was a special individual with a unique vision to communicate and with special insights to communicate through his poetry.

The key characteristics of Romantic poetry in English are:

- a reverence for, and veneration of, the natural world.
- a belief that the poet was a special person who had important truths to communicate and whose experiences were more intense than those of ordinary people.
- an emphasis on individualism and intense emotion.

- an increased interest in ordinary people – the rural poor and the urban working classes.
- a political radicalism, best summed up by the watchwords of the French Revolution – liberty, fraternity, equality.
- an overwhelming emphasis on the sensibility and imagination of the poet.
- an interest in medieval and ancient history.
- a veneration of Shakespeare.
- a desire to be original and to reject the orthodoxies of the immediate past.

Of course, not all the poets that we label 'Romantic' displayed all these characteristics all through their careers.

A Romantic Poem?

Three key features of 'London' make it a typical Romantic poem. Blake's political stance – radical, revolutionary and anti-authoritarian – tie in perfectly with the Romantic desire for political change and reform. His hostile attitude to the Church, the State and the monarchy. In the poem the speaker is identified as different from his fellow citizens – he sees and hears things that they ignore: this marks the Romantic poet as a visionary, a seer with insights which he must communicate to his fellow citizens through his art. Finally, Blake's choice of the ballad stanza – a form originally associated with anonymous medieval writing – also demonstrates Blake's egalitarian credentials. Yet Blake puts the ballad form to a new use: traditionally ballads were a narrative form – poems that told stories – but Blake presents a series of insights into the inequalities of the London of his day.

Why?

This very famous poem is remarkable.

- It is a political poem of protest against the authorities.

- This sense of protest makes it an angry and bitter poem.

- It is typically Romantic in its concern for freedom and equality, and its anti-authoritarian stance.

- Blake speaks up for the marginalized in his society.

- It uses the ballad form in a revolutionary way.

- It is remarkable for its compression of language. Blake manages to pack so much meaning into so few words.

- Its use of simple repetition, sound effects and oxymoronic imagery make it memorable and striking.

Here is the second poem that we will look at as an unseen - also by William Blake:

The Sick Rose

O rose, thou art sick!
  The invisible worm,
That flies in the night,
  In the howling storm,

Has found out thy bed   5
  Of crimson joy,
And his dark secret love
  Does thy life destroy

thou – you

thy - your

Who? The voice of the poet, the invisible worm, a rose.

When? In the night during a storm.

Where? Hard to say... in the bed of the rose.

What? Just using what we know from the poem, we can say that an invisible worm discovers the dark secret love of the rose and destroys it during a storm.

It is obvious that this method will not get us very far with this type of poem or, at least, will not get us beyond a superficial interpretation of what it means. Before you read any further, please read my comments below about William Blake's poem 'London', because Blake is also the author of 'The Sick Rose'.

What can we say with any certainty about this poem? Its mood is sinister. It is night-time and there is a howling storm. An invisible worm has found out where the rose has its bed and is coming to take its life. *Found out* suggests that the bed needs to be hidden. Paradoxically, although the worm is going to destroy the life of the rose, the worm has a *dark secret love* for the rose: this is now especially disturbing – a love which is dark and secret and which is destructive of life. Not only is it night and, therefore, dark, but the love of the worm is also dark and secret and destructive. We expect love to be a positive emotion which brings good things to our lives.

When faced with this poem many readers want to interpret the poem symbolically – otherwise it becomes a poem about horticulture. The poem is full of words that we associate with love - *rose, bed, joy, love.* In addition, in our culture sending someone roses, especially red roses, is a token of love. But this is a love which has gone wrong and is destructive. Many readers also find the shape of the worm rather phallic – suggestive of the penis. Think of all the types of love which might be considered 'wrong' or destructive. This is the list I came up with, but I am sure you can think of many others:

- Love for someone who does not love you back.

- Love for someone who is already married or in a relationship.

- Love which cannot be expressed.

- Love that transmits disease through unprotected sex.

- Love between two people from different religions.

- Love which is against the law.

- Love which is unwanted by the person you love.

- Love between two people of different class backgrounds.

- Love between two people of the same gender.

- Love or sexual expressions of love which are condemned by the church or by religious doctrine or law.

- Love which is possessive and selfish.

The point of this list is really to show that Blake's power of compression suggests a love that has gone wrong and leaves us to interpret it. To say that 'The Sick Rose' is about any one of the situations listed above would be totally wrong; to say that it suggests them all and encompasses them all, suggests the power of Blake's writing.

Furthermore, if you have read 'London' and if you remember that the rose is the national symbol of England, then this poem becomes even more than a poem about love gone wrong – it becomes (perhaps) a poem about the state of England and a warning that it will soon be destroyed. You don't have to identify exactly what or who the worm is – the poem does that for you: the worm is destructive and capable of killing – it is a symbol of ALL the things Blake hated in his society. Blake's point is that the rose is sick and is about to be destroyed by sinister, invisible powers.

Finally, if you need any proof of Blake's power to compress meaning, just look at how many words I have used in an attempt to give meaning to his words: Blake uses (including the title) only thirty-seven! This is part of the poem's power and art – that it uses powerful words and imagery from which we can extract a multitude of meanings.

Why? This astonishingly compressed and darkly evocative poem is

- a protest about the England that Blake lived in.

- a protest about the way the church and society saw certain types of love as wrong.

- a warning that love – or what we call love- can be destructive if it is not fulfilled.

My choice of two Blake poems to use in this introduction was deliberate: 'The Garden of Love' by Blake is one of the set poems in the Anthology, and one can learn more about a particular poet by reading some of his other works. Just by reading this introduction and the rest of the book you will have read three poems by William Blake – and Blake is a poet whose ideas can be hard to fully appreciate. This is one way in which you can help yourself – read poems by the poets whose poems are in the Anthology, because it will improve your understanding of the set poem. A quick internet search will throw up many poems by the set poets and, where appropriate, I have made a suggestion for further reading at the end of each commentary.

I have chosen to include the next poem because it is a famous poem about love and, in what I have written about it, I have used quotations from critics who have expressed views on the poem. An awareness of critical views is part of the progression from GCSE to A level. Assessment 5 at English A Level is to 'explore literary texts informed by different interpretations'. This does not mean that you need to use quotations from critics, but, where appropriate, in the commentary to each poem I have attempted to put forward a different view from the prevailing consensus about a particular poem.

'Porphyria's Lover' – Robert Browning

The rain set early in to-night,
    The sullen wind was soon awake,
It tore the elm-tops down for spite,
    And did its worst to vex the lake:
    I listened with heart fit to break.
When glided in Porphyria; straight
    She shut the cold out and the storm,

And kneeled and made the cheerless grate
    Blaze up, and all the cottage warm;
    Which done, she rose, and from her form
Withdrew the dripping cloak and shawl,
    And laid her soiled gloves by, untied
Her hat and let the damp hair fall,
    And, last, she sat down by my side
    And called me. When no voice replied,
She put my arm about her waist,
    And made her smooth white shoulder bare,
And all her yellow hair displaced,
    And, stooping, made my cheek lie there,
    And spread, o'er all, her yellow hair,
Murmuring how she loved me — she
    Too weak, for all her heart's endeavour,
To set its struggling passion free
    From pride, and vainer ties dissever,
    And give herself to me for ever.
But passion sometimes would prevail,
    Nor could to-night's gay feast restrain
A sudden thought of one so pale
    For love of her, and all in vain:
    So, she was come through wind and rain.
Be sure I looked up at her eyes
    Happy and proud; at last I knew
Porphyria worshipped me; surprise
    Made my heart swell, and still it grew
    While I debated what to do.
That moment she was mine, mine, fair,
    Perfectly pure and good: I found
A thing to do, and all her hair
    In one long yellow string I wound

Three times her little throat around,
And strangled her. No pain felt she;
    I am quite sure she felt no pain.
As a shut bud that holds a bee,
    I warily oped her lids: again
    Laughed the blue eyes without a stain.
And I untightened next the tress
    About her neck; her cheek once more
Blushed bright beneath my burning kiss:
    I propped her head up as before,
    Only, this time my shoulder bore
Her head, which droops upon it still:
    The smiling rosy little head,
So glad it has its utmost will,
    That all it scorned at once is fled,
    And I, its love, am gained instead!
Porphyria's love: she guessed not how
    Her darling one wish would be heard.
And thus we sit together now,
    And all night long we have not stirred,
    And yet God has not said a word!

Context

Robert Browning was born in 1812 and became one of the most famous English poets of the Victorian era. He was married to Elizabeth Barrett Browning who was a semi-invalid with an over-protective father. The couple were married in secret and then went to live in Italy. Browning's best work is often set in the past and he was a master of the dramatic monologue, in which the imagined speaker of the poem reveals their innermost thoughts and feelings, often going on to uncover uncomfortable truths about themselves.

porphyria – a rare disorder of the blood that may cause mental, nervous or skin problems.

vex – annoy, anger.

soiled – dirty, unclean.

dissever – to separate, to part in two.

oped – opened.

tress – a long lock of hair.

Who? The poem is a dramatic monologue spoken by the male lover of Porphyria.

When? One dark stormy might. Browning uses the weather as a pathetic fallacy for the turbulent human emotions in the cottage.

Where? In an isolated cottage.

What? The speaker, without a word of explanation or regret, tells of Porphyria's visit to him and his subsequent murder of her. The speaker spends the night alone with the body of his dead lover.

Commentary

'Porphyria's Lover' by Robert Browning dramatizes the conflicts between social pressures and romantic love; the tension between female submissiveness and the male urge to possess, to control and to act; the tension between momentary pleasure and the human need to preserve and keep that transitory pleasure; and the tension between strong religious faith and religious doubt.

In 'Porphyria's Lover' Browning presents a speaker who is insane. The poem was originally published in 1836 in the London journal

Monthly Repository (Hawlin, 44) and was paired with another poem with an identical rhyme scheme, metre, line length and overall length (Ryals, 166). The paired poems were printed under the title 'Madhouse Cells' and the other poem, 'Johannes Agricola in Meditation', shares a similar preoccupation to 'Porphyria's Lover' – what Ryals calls the desire or will for 'total possession of another person' (166).

The poem is a dramatic monologue – a type of poem that Browning would continue to write throughout his career, but in this early example the monologue seems to be addressed to the reader; later dramatic monologues, such as 'My Last Duchess' and 'Fra Lippo Lippi' where Browning developed the form by including within the poem other characters to whom the monologue is addressed (Ryals, 87). In 'Porphyria's Lover' the speaker is isolated in many ways as we will see. The speaker is recounting the events of the previous evening, so the poem is written after the main event of the poem (which Browning, as the poet, cleverly delays until line 42.). The speaker – the lover of Porphyria – has a tender tone as he recounts the events of the previous evening: indeed, Hawlin comments that his 'whole perspective is… gentle or feminized' (46). However, the speaker is also mad, and the crucial event of the poem in line 42, throws his previous solicitude and apparent love and care for Porphyria into a dark and deadly ironic light.

Browning's monologues are frequently voiced by eccentrics, lunatics, or people under emotional stress. Their ramblings illustrate character by describing the interactions of an odd personality with a particularly telling set of circumstances. In both 'Porphyria's Lover' and 'My Last Duchess', Browning uses this mode of exposition to describe a man who responds to the love of a beautiful woman by killing her. Each monologue offers the speakers' reasons for the desired woman from subject to object: in 'My Last Duchess', the Duke may have jealously murdered his wife, but keeps a portrait of her behind a curtain so none can look upon her smile without his permission; in 'Porphyria's Lover', the persona wishes to stop time at a single perfect moment and so kills his lover and sits all night embracing her carefully arranged body. It should be noted that in 'My Last Duchess' the woman's murder is at best implied, while in 'Porphyria's Lover' it is described quite explicitly by the speaker. The unchanging rhythmic pattern may also suggest the persona's insanity.

The 'Porphyria' persona's romantic egotism leads him into all manner of monstrously selfish assumptions compatible with his own longings. He seems convinced that Porphyria wanted to be murdered, and claims 'No pain felt she' while being strangled, adding, as if to convince himself, 'I am quite sure she felt no pain.' He may even believe she enjoyed the pain, because he, her lover, inflicted it. When she's dead, he says she's found her 'utmost will,' and when he sees her lifeless head drooping on his shoulder, he describes it as a 'smiling rosy little head', possibly using the word 'rosy' to symbolise the red roses of love, or to demonstrate his delusion that the girl, and their relationship, are still alive. More likely, however, is the thought that blood returning to her face, after the strangulation, makes her cheeks 'rosy.' Her 'rosy little head' may also be a sly reference to the hymen; Porphyria leaves a 'gay feast' and comes in from the outside world wearing 'soiled gloves'; now her blue eyes, open in death, are 'without a stain.' The lover may also be a fetishist, indicated by the fact that he refers to her hair numerous times throughout the poem, and strangles her with it. He also refers to the 'shut bud that holds a bee' which backs up the view of it being a sexual fetish.

It is impossible to know the true nature of his relationship to Porphyria. An incestuous relationship has been suggested; Porphyria might be the speaker's mother or sister. Another possibility is that she is a former lover, now betrothed, or even married, to some other man. Alternatively, they may be divided by social class.

Other sources speculate that the lover might be impotent, disabled, sick, or otherwise inadequate, and, as such, unable to satisfy Porphyria. There is much textual evidence to support this interpretation: he describes himself as 'one so pale / for love of her, and all in vain.' At the beginning of the poem, the persona never moves; he sits passively in a cold, dark room, sadly listening to the storm until Porphyria comes through 'wind and rain', 'shuts the cold out and the storm,' and makes up his dying fire. Finally, she sits beside him, calls his name, places his arm around her waist, and puts his head on her shoulder; interestingly, she has to stoop to do this. She is active; he is passive – suggesting impotence perhaps. At the poem's midpoint, the persona suddenly takes action, strangling Porphyria, propping her body against his, and boasting that afterwards, *her* head lay on *his* shoulder.

In line with the persona's suggested weakness and sickness, other scholars take the word 'porphyria' literally, and suggest that the seductress embodies a disease, and that the persona's killing of her is a sign of his recovery. Porphyria, which usually involved delusional madness and death, was classified several years before the poem's publication; Browning, who had an avid interest in such pathologies, may well have been aware of the new disease, and used it in this way to express his knowledge.

Much has been made of the final line: 'And yet, God has not said a word!' Possibly, the speaker seeks divine approval for the murder. He may believe God has said nothing because He is satisfied with his actions. God may be satisfied because: He recognises that the persona's crime is the only way to keep Porphyria pure; or, because He doesn't think her life and death are important compared to the persona's. The persona may also be waiting in vain for some sign of God's approval. Alternatively, the line may represent his feelings of emptiness in the wake of his violence; Porphyria is gone, quiet descends, and he's alone. The persona may also be schizophrenic; he may be listening for a voice in his head, which he mistakes for the voice of God. It has also been postulated that this is Browning's statement of 'God's silence,' in which neither good nor bad acts are immediately recompensed by the deity.

The final line may also register the persona's sense of guilt over his crime. Despite his elaborate justifications for his act, he has, in fact, committed murder, and he expects God to punish him – or, at least, to take notice. The persona is surprised, perhaps a little uneasy, at God's continued silence. An alternative reading of the last line is to identify a slightly gleeful tone in it – confirming once again that the speaker is insane.

There is no doubt of his insanity; exactly why he kills Porphyria is open to debate and interpretation.

The poem is set in an isolated rural cottage: Browning implies this because Porphyria who has walked through a storm to meet her lover is completely wet and immediately takes off her 'dripping cloak and shawl' (line 11) and her 'soiled gloves' (line 12). Browning uses the storm as a pathetic fallacy in at least three ways: firstly, it is an effective contrast with the warmth and love within the cottage once Porphyria lights the fire and makes advances to her lover; secondly, it can be seen as Browning foreshadowing the later, violent events of the poem; and, thirdly, it might even be seen as symbolizing the tortured inner feelings of Porphyria's 'murderously jealous lover' (Hair & Kennedy, 88) — feelings which he keeps under careful control. Knoepflmacher argues that Browning presents very well the 'contrast between a cold outside world and a warm interior' (158) and Porphyria herself can be seen as 'the passionate outsider penetrating that interior who brings warmth to the immobile dreamer within' (158). However, this can be seen as an example of prolepsis, since, despite the speaker's self-delusional assertions, in death Porphyria's body will rapidly lose all its warmth.

The relationship between the two lovers is presented by Browning as a clandestine one, but one which Porphyria wants: she has, after all, braved a storm to visit her lover and the way she 'put my arm about her waist,/And made her smooth white shoulder bare' (lines 16 -17) clearly suggests that the relationship is sexual. It seems that Browning suggests that it has to be clandestine because Porphyria and her lover are from different classes: Martens asserts that the poem is essentially about a man's 'pathological love for a socially-superior woman' (39). Browning suggests this through the speaker's words: he says that Porphyria is 'too weak… from pride' (lines 22 & 24) – presumably a pride issuing from her social superiority and the disgrace she would suffer if her love for this man became known, and he goes on to say that she is 'too weak' (line 22) to allow her 'struggling passion free' (line 23) and 'give herself to me forever' (line 25), because she is socially bound by what the speaker dismisses as 'vainer ties' (line 24) – presumably her sense of responsibility to her family. Browning presents the speaker as being very distraught at this situation: it explains why he does not respond in line 15 when she calls him and he comments that, because he cannot have her forever or is dependent on her secret visits to him, it seems that his love for her is 'all in vain' (line 30). But passion prevails – Browning hints perhaps that they make love and, as they do so, the man notices how Porphyria is looking at him and realizes 'I knew/Porphyria worshipped me' (lines 33 -34). He goes on: 'That moment she was mine, mine, fair,/Perfectly pure and good' (line 38). But it is only a moment of intense feeling and, given what Browning has suggested about the nature of their relationship and his dependence on her coming to him when she can and not when she or he both want, he decides to preserve the moment and strangles her with her own hair. The repeated 'mine, mine' in line 37 convey his extreme possessiveness and Knoepflmacher writes that 'by draining Porphyria of her life, he can assume… control' (160). This can easily be seen as symptomatic of the masculine desire to possess and control, the human desire to preserve forever a moment of happiness, and we might even see the speaker as rebelling against a rigid class system which keeps him and his lover apart. However, by killing Porphyria, Browning presents the insane speaker as having wholly abrogated all moral responsibility for his actions and acted in defiance of human law and morality.

Mirroring the speaker's desire for control, the poem's structure is highly controlled. On the page the poem looks highly regular and it is: Browning conveys his speaker's thoughts with a regular unvarying rhyme scheme which consists of units of six lines which rhyme ABABB, CDCDD and so on. This tightly-controlled and very regular rhyme scheme could be said to mirror the speaker's own need for control and his obsession with Porphyria; at the same time, despite the horrific nature of his crime, his speaking voice remains calm and untroubled – just as the poem is very formally and regularly structured. Hawlin (42) describes the rhyme scheme as 'assymetrical'

– presumably meaning that we might expect the six line unit to rhyme like this – ABABAB – but the rhyme scheme that Browning has chosen with the fifth and sixth line rhyming with each other, means that in terms of rhyme, the six line unit turns back on itself – an attempt surely to accentuate the self-obsessed, inward-looking nature of the speaker. In other words, the speaker is concerned only with his own feelings, despite his apparent concern for Porphyria – (No pain felt she;/I am quite sure she felt no pain' (lines 42 – 43). As Bailey asserts, the speaker has a 'megalomaniac stance towards his lover' (53), and he is 'self-deceiving' (Hair & Kennedy, 88). This self-deception and the evidence of his insanity continues after Porphyria is dead: the speaker thinks that her eyes 'laughed… without a stain' (line 46) and that 'her cheek once more/Blushed bright beneath my burning kiss' (lines 48 -49).

Browning uses a lot of enjambment – twenty-two times in a poem of sixty lines - so that over a third of the lines run on and are not end-stopped. On the one hand, it could be said that this enjambment helps convey the impression of a real voice that is speaking, but there is perhaps another purpose: in so many lines the words and syntax break through the end of the line and this is a poem about a speaker who breaks accepted morality by committing murder. Furthermore, the lines which build up to and describe Porphyria's murder – lines 32 to 42 – use an excessive amount of enjambment which perhaps help to convey the speaker's frenzy, emphasize his breaking of the rules and quicken the rhythm of the poem to its climax, as well as imitating the speedy act of strangling his lover. Browning's use of heavy, full-stop caesuras is equally significant. He uses only two: one in line 15 after Prophyria 'sat down by my side/And called me.' (lines 14 – 15) – a caesura which is used to emphasize the speaker's lack of response to her; the second in line 42 after 'strangled her' – which again serves, for the reader, to emphasize the enormity of the crime he has committed. The caesura helps to foreground the act of murder. However, Browning presents the speaker as so delusional that he argues that in killing his lover he was doing what she would have wanted: he describes her head as 'so glad it has its utmost will' (line 54) and he claims in his insanity that his killing of her is 'her darling one wish' (line 58). The speaker's final observation – that on the subject of the murder 'God has not said a word!' (line 60) – certainly shows the speaker's contempt and insouciance towards religious diktats forbidding murder.

Browning's 'Porphyria's Lover' is a deeply disturbing poem, enhanced by the strict regularity of the rhyme scheme and the control that Browning exerts over it. What appears to be a passionate story of the secret tryst of two lovers turns into a tale of sudden and violent murder, and a crazed and deluded justification of it. Ryals states that 'there has been some disagreement as to whether the lover kills Porphyria because he loves her or hates her' (271): it could be argued that such a question is irrelevant because, love her or hate her, he seeks to possess her completely and forever. It can be seen that the poem raises other issues – the unfairness of the British class system, the habitual, historical male need to dominate and a growing scepticism about God – but these are overshadowed by the pathological and wholly solipsistic megalomania of the speaker.

Works Cited

Bailey, Suzanne. *Cognitive Style and Perceptual Difference in Browning's Poetry*. London: Routledge, 2010. Print.

Browning, Robert. 'Porphyria's Lover'. *Poetry Foundation*. Web. October 28th, 2013.

Hair, Donald S. & Kennedy, Richard S. *The Dramatic Imagination of Robert Browning: A Literary Life*. Columbia, Mi: University of Missouri Press, 2007. Print.

Hawlin, Stefan. *Robert Browning*. London: Routledge, 2012. Print.

Knoepflmacher, U. C. 'Projection of the Female Other: Romanticism, Browning and the Victorian Dramatic Monologue'. Pp. 147 – 168 in Claridge, Laura & Langland, Elizabeth (eds.). *Out of Bounds: Male Writers and Gendered Criticism*. Boston, Ma: University of Massachusetts Press, 1990. Print.

Martens, Britta. *Browning, Victorian Poetics and the Romantic Legacy: Challenging the Personal Voice*. London: Aldgate Publishing Ltd, 2011. Print.

Ryals, Clyde de L. *Robert Browning: The Poems and Plays of Robert Browning, 1833 – 1846*. Columbus, Oh: Ohio State University Press, 1983. Print.

In 'Porphyria's Lover' Browning:

- uses dramatic monologue to present a solipsistic, psychopathic maniac;

- to suggest an illicit love affair, perhaps caused by social differences;

- uses a rigid rhyme scheme and metre to suggest the speaker's confidence and rigidity of thinking, but also uses caesura brilliantly at key moments;

- presents an insane mind obsessed with full possession of his lover;

- in the poem presents possessive love as a life-denying force.

Rhythm and Scansion

Before we examine our final poem we must consider the question of rhythm in poetry. To be able to write about rhythm with understanding and sensitivity at A level is an essential skill. It is not enough to state that Marvell's "To His Coy Mistress" is written in iambic tetrameters – that proves nothing and adds nothing to our appreciation of the poem – but to have an ear that can spot when Marvell varies the iambic rhythm is a skill that can be learnt and also allows you to make a critical point about why Marvell chooses to vary the rhythm when he does. I cannot stress enough too that you should get in the habit of reading poems aloud.

The definition of poetry that I quoted above said that the pattern of poetry is *almost always a rhythm or metre*. Rhythm and metre depend on the words chosen by the poet and the length of the line and they depend, to a very large extent, on the ways we say words in real life. When we pronounce any English word of two syllables of more we put the accent or stress or emphasis on only one syllable.

Let us choose a simple example. A desert (as you know) is a large, sandy area largely barren of life; a dessert is a pudding, the sweet course at the end of a meal. Of course, we distinguish between them in writing by writing dessert (the pudding) with a double 's'. But we also pronounce them differently – and when we pronounce them differently, and the different pronunciation is to do with which syllable we stress: in '**des**ert' the first syllable is stressed (which is why I have emboldened it and underlined it); in 'dess**ert**' we stress the second syllable.

Another example: a comet is lump of rock hurtling in outer space; to commit is a verb. But while the sound of the two words is similar the real difference when we say them is that we pronounce the first syllable of '**com**et' and the second syllable of 'com**mit**'.

I have used these examples from normal speech to show you that stress is not something confined to poetry, but something that has a bearing on how we pronounce words in everyday life.

There is a lot to learn about metre, but when it comes to English poetry we can get away with knowing about just four forms which either build up or totter down and are said to be rising or falling. This is how metrical patterns work:

IAMBIC METRE – unstress, stress

ANAPAESTIC METRE – unstress, unstress, stress

TROCHAIC METRE – stress, unstress

DACTYLIC METRE – stress, unstress, unstress

And it helps to be aware of two others which are rare in English poetry, but do turn up once in a while:

SPONDAIC METRE – stress, stress

PYRRHIC METRE - unstress, unstress

When you come across them you term them

an iamb or an iambic foot

a trochee or a trochaic foot

an anapaest or an anapaestic foot

a spondee or a spondaic foot

a pyrrhus or a pyrric foot.

The metre is then divided into feet – with one foot generally having one stressed syllable – and the metre is described according to the number of feet or stresses in each line:

MONOMETER – one stress

DIMETER – two stresses

TRIMETER – three stresses

TETRAMETER – four stresses

PENTAMETER – five stresses

HEXAMETER – six stresses

HEPTAMETER – seven stresses

OCTAMETER - eight stresses

However, as Philip Hobsbaum says in his book *Metre, Rhythm and Verse Form*:

...many practising poets would question whether much to do with 'art'. They are primarily a matter of craft....Metre is a blueprint; rhythm is the inhabited building. Metre is a skeleton; rhythm is the functioning body. Metre is a map; rhythm is a land.

For example, in the commentaries below we shall discover that Andrew Marvell's 'To His Coy Mistress' is written in iambic tetrameters, but what is most interesting is where Marvell uses metrical variation by using a trochaic foot or a spondaic foot to reflect the meaning of the words or to foreground some words or phrases. We will see other examples of where the poet departs from the overriding metrical scheme to add variety or to enhance the impact of the words. These metrical variations are foregrounded BECAUSE they break the pattern. One of the most common metrical variations is starting a line with a trochaic foot in a predominately iambic poem.

In English poetry the most common metre is the iambic foot and the most common line length is the pentameter ('pent' is for five because there are five stresses in the line, ten syllables in all) and this gives a tee-tum rhythm as in

And **one** and **two** and **three** and **four** and **five**.

Or this first line by Rupert Brooke (1887 – 1915), which is a perfect iambic pentameter (five feet, comprising ten syllables with the stress on each second one):

If **I** should **die** think **on**ly **this** of **me**.

Metre is always worth looking at closely, because when you do, you find a sense the poet intended which may have been lost down the ages. Take Hamlet's most famous soliloquy – 'To be or not to be, that is the question'. This is an iambic pentameter except with an extra syllable to represent Hamlet's distress and uncertainty – so it is in the metrical variation that much interest lies. [Strictly speaking the line should have 10 syllables, not the 11 that Shakespeare uses – but poets like breaking rules!]

Because iambic rhythm is the one that comes closest to the natural rhythm of English speech it pops up in prose too – as in the opening sentence of Dickens' *A Tale of Two Cities* (which we used earlier to exemplify parallelism and repetition):

It **was** the **best** of **times**; it **was** the **worst** of **times**.

Dickens' sentence is perfectly iambic. Rhythm exists in ordinary speech too: *Teenage Mutant Ninja Turtles* and *Monty Python's Flying Circus* are both examples of trochaic tetrameter, while my own name is a trochaic dimeter – **Da**vid **Whee**ler.

Trochaic metre reverses the stress, so we end up with a TUM-tee rhythm much beloved of William Blake. Where an iambic rhythm tends to be reflective, trochaic rhythm is more assertive so we get

ONE and TWO and THREE and FOUR and FIVE and

Or as the way Longfellow used trochaic metre in *Hiawatha*:

By the **shin**ing **big** sea **wat**er

William Blake's Introduction to his Songs of Innocence in 1789 shows just what you can do with trochaic metre. The poem is a trochais trimeter (lines of trochees in three feet) with an added stressed syllable at the end of each line which seems to just dangle there until you realise the importance of this stressed extra word:

Piping **down** the **vall**eys **wild**

Piping **songs** of **pleas**ant **glee**

The two words which stand out in these lines are wild and glee and Blake is able to draw attention to their extraordinary contrast by placing them at the end of the lines with a heavy stress on them. The *valleys wild* – normal speech would have *wild valleys*, but because you lose the stress you can see why that wouldn't have worked – conjures up the image of a dangerous place where we ought to tread warily, but in his innocence, the piper sees none of that as he skips about the *valleys wild* and pipes *songs of pleasant glee*. The reader, of course, gets a sense of foreboding from this introduction of the horrors to come – which they do in *Songs of Experience*.

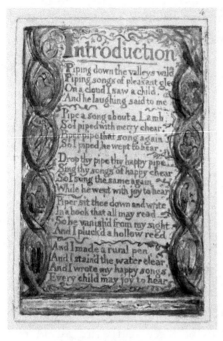

Changing the natural word-order from 'wild valleys' to 'valleys wild' is known as inversion and is normally used to make a rhyme fit. But this poetic device makes the language stilted and unnatural which is why it is rarely practised by modern poets who favour sticking to the word order of natural speech.

Also take a look at the last stanza of the Introduction. On first reading it seems as if the word *I* should be the most important, but the meter dictates otherwise.

And I **made** a **rur**al **pen**

And I **stained** the **wat**er **clear**

And I **wrote** my **hap**py **songs**

Every **child** may **joy** to **hear**.

It's the additional things the piper gets up to which should be catching our attention which is why the stress falls on *and*. Here he is surrounded by fresh, clear water and what does he do? He pollutes it with ink, giving a slight sense of foreboding about what is to come later in *Songs of Experience* and adding a vaguely ironic quality to some of the *Songs of Innocence*. Here is the whole poem:

Piping down the valleys wild
Piping songs of pleasant glee
On a cloud I saw a child.

And he laughing said to me.

Pipe a song about a Lamb;
So I piped with merry chear,
Piper pipe that song again—
So I piped, he wept to hear.

Drop thy pipe thy happy pipe
Sing thy songs of happy chear,
So I sung the same again
While he wept with joy to hear,

Piper sit thee down and write
In a book that all may read—
So he vanish'd from my sight.
And I pluck'd a hollow reed.

And I made a rural pen,
And I stain'd the water clear,
And I wrote my happy songs
Every child may joy to hear.

The next two metres, anapaestic and dactylic, are trisyllabic feet – they have three syllables – a sort of extension of the disyllabic feet of iambs and trochees. But iambic and anapaestic feet readily mix in the same poem because they have the same stress patterns, as do trochaic and dactylic. Anapaests gallop quickly, while dactyls slow you to a quiet walk of regret and are perfectly suited to sad or troubled emotions.

In anapaestic metre the stress falls on the last syllable of the foot – as it does with iambic – so what you get is

And a ONE and a TWO and a THREE and a FOUR and a FIVE.

Or as in these lines in anapaestic tetrameter by Byron (1788 – 1824) in the poem 'The Destruction of Sennacherib':

The As**syr**ian came **down** like the **wolf** on the **fold**,
And his **co**horts were **gleam**ing in **pur**ple and **gold**;
And the **sheen** of their **spears** was like **stars** on the **sea**,
When the **blue** wave rolls **night**ly on **deep** Gali**lee**.

  Like the leaves of the forest when Summer is green,
That host with their banners at sunset were seen:
Like the leaves of the forest when Autumn hath blown,
That host on the morrow lay withered and strown.

  For the Angel of Death spread his wings on the blast,
And breathed in the face of the foe as he passed;
And the eyes of the sleepers waxed deadly and chill,
And their hearts but once heaved, and for ever grew still!

  And there lay the steed with his nostril all wide,
But through it there rolled not the breath of his pride;
And the foam of his gasping lay white on the turf,
And cold as the spray of the rock-beating surf.

  And there lay the rider distorted and pale,
With the dew on his brow, and the rust on his mail:
And the tents were all silent, the banners alone,
The lances unlifted, the trumpet unblown.

  And the widows of Ashur are loud in their wail,
And the idols are broke in the temple of Baal;
And the might of the Gentile, unsmote by the sword,
Hath melted like snow in the glance of the Lord!

By using this metre Byron is creating a sense of expectancy with the rising nature of the stress coming at the end of the foot. We want to know what the Assyrian is going to do next. There are other things going on this poem, all enhanced by the anapaestic rhythm. Firstly, when read aloud the poem generates a quick speed which is very appropriate for a narrative poem full of action – the rhythm pushes us on to the next stage of the story. Secondly and more importantly, the speed mimics the speed of the Assyrian army as it approaches Jerusalem – it may even be said to mimic the speed and rhythm of the horses of its army approaching. Thirdly, and perhaps most important of all, the rhythm and its speed suggest the speed of the Assyrian defeat and devastation at the hands of the Angel of Death. In general, therefore, the rhythm helps give us an aural sense of the urgency of the situation facing Jerusalem and the speed at which the events unfold.

The rhyme scheme is AABB: the first two lines in each stanza rhyme with each other as do the third and fourth lines. This apposition of lines is powerful and suggests the opposition between the invading Assyrian army and Jerusalem and its defenders. Byron also uses anaphora at the start of many of his lines – 'like', 'then' and 'and' – 'then' and 'and' are especially appropriate in a narrative poem describing a quick series of events.

While anapaestic rhythm builds up emotion because of its rising rhythm, dactylic metre tends to be sad because of its falling rhythm – TUM-tee-tee. Anapaests can whip up tension by rushing the reader through the unstressed syllables to land on the stressed one, whereas dactyls create a sense of decline and falling away by hitting you with the first stressed syllable and then tailing off with the two subsequent ones as the metre tapers away. As in Thomas Hood's (1799-1845) *Bridge of Sighs*:

Take her up **ten**derly
Fashioned so **slen**derly
Or
Touch her not **scorn**fully
Think of her **mourn**fully

Or Robert Browning's (1812-1869) *The Lost Leader* about the appointment of William Wordsworth as Poet Laureate in1843. The young, headstrong and rebellious Browning was furious with Wordsworth for accepting the post – *a riband to stick in his coat* – because it seemed a betrayal of everything Wordsworth had previously stood for which is why he becomes The Lost Leader of the title. Wordsworth was no longer the leader of the young poets of the day like Browning, who were disgusted because they felt he had sold out. A rebel and radical in his youth, Wordsworth had finally succumbed to the Establishment. He'd already upset Browning by accepting a Government pension – a handful of silver – which showed his growing conservatism. But taking the Poet Laureate's job (a government sinecure) was the last straw for Browning as you can see from this extract in dactylic tetrameter with one or two stressed syllables at the end of some lines to re-inforce his point.

THE LOST LEADER

Just for a handful of silver he left us,
    Just for a riband to stick in his coat—
Found the one gift of which fortune bereft us,
    Lost all the others she lets us devote;
They, with the gold to give, doled him out silver,
    So much was theirs who so little allowed:
How all our copper had gone for his service!

Rags—were they purple, his heart had been proud!
We that had loved him so, followed him, honoured him,
    Lived in his mild and magnificent eye,
Learned his great language, caught his clear accents,
    Made him our pattern to live and to die!
Shakespeare was of us, Milton was for us,
    Burns, Shelley, were with us,—they watch from their graves!
He alone breaks from the van and the freemen,
    —He alone sinks to the rear and the slaves!

Because this is a poem of sadness and regret, the heavy, mournful dactyls are totally appropriate to the theme giving us the rhythm of

ONE two three ONE two three ONE two three ONE two

As in:

We that had **loved** him so, **foll**owed him, **hon**oured him.
Lived in his **mild** and mag**ni**ficent **eye**.

The falling rhythm that the predominantly dactylic metre sets up often produces a melancholic, poignant and sad atmosphere in English poetry.

The spondee or spondaic foot has two long stressed syllables as in *door mat*. The spondee is often used to add emphasis or to foreground certain words in predominately iambic or trochaic poems – to add metrical variation. It is rare for a whole poem to consist of spondees but Ted Hughes uses spondees freely to suggest dead weight in this extract from his *View of a Pig*:

The **pig lay** on the **barrow dead**.
It **weighed**, they **said**, as **much** as **three men**.

Its **eyes closed**, **pink white eyelash**es.
Its **trot**ters **stuck straight out**.

Finally

THE VOICE

Thomas Hardy

Woman much missed, how you call to me, call to me,
Saying that now you are not as you were
When you had changed from the one who was all to me,
But as at first, when our day was fair.

Can it be you that I hear? Let me view you, then,
Standing as when I drew near to the town
Where you would wait for me: yes, as I knew you then,
Even to the original air-blue gown!

Or is it only the breeze, in its listlessness
Travelling across the wet mead to me here,
You being ever dissolved to wan wistlessness,
Heard no more again far or near?

    Thus I; faltering forward,
    Leaves around me falling,
Wind oozing thin through the thorn from norward,
    And the woman calling.

Context

listlessness – the state of being listless, lacking energy.

mead – meadow or field.

wan – pale.

wistlessness – 'to wist' is an old English verb meaning to know. So 'wistlessness' is literally the state of being no longer known.

Who? The poet speaks as himself, addressing his dead wife.

When? After his wife's death. The poem comes from a sequence known as *Poems 1912-13*.

Where? An outdoor setting suggested by the final stanza, the wet mead and the wind and the falling leaves.

What? The poet is haunted by the voice of his dead wife and he reminiscences about how happy they were at the start of their relationship. The final stanza breaks the pattern of the previous three stanzas to suggest Hardy's forlorn sadness, his heart-felt confusion and his lack of direction.

Before we can get to grips with this poem we need to know something about Hardy's personal life. In 1870, while on an architectural mission to restore the parish church of St Juliot in Cornwall (he was a trained architect), Hardy met and fell in love with Emma Lavinia Gifford, whom he married in 1874. In 1885 Thomas and his wife moved into Max Gate, a house Hardy had designed himself and his brother had built. Although they later became estranged and the love between them faded, her subsequent death in 1912 had a traumatic effect on him and after her death, Hardy made a trip to Cornwall to revisit places linked with their courtship; his *Poems 1912–13* reflect upon her death. In 1914, Hardy married his secretary Florence Emily Dugdale, who was 39 years his junior. However, he remained preoccupied with his first wife's death and tried to overcome his remorse by writing poetry. 'The Voice' is one of the most celebrated poems about his dead wife.

In the first stanza Hardy imagines the voice of his dead wife calling him. The first line is metrically very complex. It starts arrestingly with a trochaic foot – 'woman' – which is followed by an alliterative spondee – 'much missed' before ending the line on a falling dactylic metre – 'call to me, call to me' and the repetition of the words suggests that he keeps hearing her voice in his mind. The falling dactylic metre conjures up a mood of forlorn sadness and plangent regret, and Hardy uses the same way to end the first and third lines of the first three stanzas. The rest of the first stanza uses very simple English words to describe a complex emotional situation. Hardy imagines that his dead wife, Emma, is telling him that she has changed back to the person he knew when he first met her – 'as at first, when our day was fair'. In other words, she has changed from when their marriage developed problems – when she has changed from the one who was all to him – and has changed back to her original self.

The second stanza opens with a direct question: 'Can it be you that I hear?' – which is given added force by the caesura which follows it. If he can hear her voice, he wants to see her too – 'Let me view you then.' Hardy summons up an image of Emma when they had just met and she would wait for him on the edge of town. The last three syllables of the stanza are stressed – 'air-blue gown' – which suggests the striking immediacy of Hardy's memory and its force and clarity even though he is thinking of events from decades before.

There is a radical change of tone in the third stanza and the use of pathetic fallacy to present the way Hardy is feeling. He wonders whether it is not Emma's voice that he can hear at all but

...is it only the breeze, in its listlessness
Travelling across the wet mead to me here.

The dactyl which ends line one maintains the tone of febrile frailty
and sadness: after all, Hardy knows that Emma is dead 'dissolved to
wan wistlessness' and death is final: Emma is 'Heard no more again
far or near' and the alliteration on 'w' and the sibilance of 'wan
wistlessness' contributes to a subdued sense of sadness.

The final stanza breaks completely the pattern Hardy established in
the first three: so great is his regret that he loses control of the shape
and pattern of the poem. The first line is interesting:

Thus I; faltering forward

The caesura after 'Thus I' enacts Hardy's own faltering, while the
alliteration on the soft 'f' suggests hesitation and frailty and is
continued in the 'falling' of the leaves in the next line. There is
pathetic fallacy too: it is autumn and the leaves are falling as a
precursor to winter. The north wind is blowing too so it will be very
cold. The line:
Wind oozing thin through the thorn from norward
is an interesting combination of vowel sounds with short 'i' sounds
(wind and thin) contrasting with longer 'o' (oozing, through, thorn,
norward) which suggests the wind gusting through the thick thorn
bush. There is also alliteration on 'th' – a difficult sound to say and
which stresses the effort with which the wind blows. The poem ends
where it began with 'the woman calling'.

There is something grammatically interesting about the last stanza
too: technically it is not a complete sentence because it contains no

finite verb – there is no completed action which suggests that there is no escape for Hardy from these feelings and that he will always hear Emma's voice, always regret how their marriage fell apart. All the verbs Hardy uses are non-finite, present participles – 'faltering', 'falling', 'oozing', 'calling' – which suggest a never-ending sequence of events that he cannot control (after all he is 'faltering'). Hardy also ends each line of the last stanza with a trochaic foot and this falling, feminine rhythm also contributes to its sadness.

This poem shows Hardy at the height of his powers as a poet.

Thee, Thou, Thy and Thine

Language changes all the time. The words that form the title for this section now exist only in some dialects of English and in the literature of the past. They are all ways of saying you or yours: 'thou' is 'you' (subject pronoun); 'thee' is you (object pronoun); 'thy' is 'your' (possessive adjective as in 'your or thy lover'; 'thine' is 'yours' (possessive pronoun). In the past people used 'thee' and 'thou' to their social equals or to people they were emotionally close to; they used 'you' if they were talking to more than one person OR if they were talking to a social superior or a stranger.

No one knows why 'thee' and 'thou' dropped out of use, but English has lost the ability to distinguish between degrees of intimacy amongst the people we interact with. Most European languages have kept an informal 'you' and a more formal one: French has 'tu' and 'vous', German 'du' and 'sie', Spanish 'tu' and 'usted' and Italian 'tu' and 'Lei'.

Endings

This may seem like an obvious point, one hardly worth drawing attention to, but you have seen from the poems discussed above that the endings of poem are absolutely vital and crucial to their overall effect. In 'The Sick Rose' the final word – *destroy* – carries threat and menace. You will find in many of the poems in the Anthology the ending – the final stanza, the final line, the final sentence, even sometimes the final word – changes what has gone before and forces us to see things differently. So be aware of this as you read and as you revise. When you are writing about poems, the way they end and the emotional conclusion they achieve is a simple way to compare and contrast them. It may not be easy to express what it is exactly that they do achieve, but make sure you write something about the endings, because the endings are often the key to the whole poem. Remember – a poem (like a song) is an emotional journey and the destination, the ending, is part of the overall message, probably its most important part.

'Whoso List to Hunt' – Sir Thomas Wyatt

Whoso list to hunt, I know where is an hind,
But as for me, *hélas*, I may no more.
The vain travail hath wearied me so sore,
I am of them that farthest cometh behind.
Yet may I by no means my wearied mind
Draw from the deer, but as she fleeth afore
Fainting I follow. I leave off therefore,
Sithens in a net I seek to hold the wind.
Who list her hunt, I put him out of doubt,
As well as I may spend his time in vain.
And graven with diamonds in letters plain
There is written, her fair neck round about:
Noli me tangere, for Caesar's I am,
And wild for to hold, though I seem tame.

Author & Context

Sir Thomas Wyatt (1503 – 11 October 1542) was a 16th-century English ambassador and lyrical poet. He was a courtier at the court of Henry VIII and he led diplomatic missions to Italy, which allowed him to become familiar with innovations in Italian poetry.

He is credited with being the first English poet to write sonnets in English, thus introducing the sonnet into English literature. He was born in Kent at Allington Castle, which is near Maidstone in Kent, though his family was originally from Yorkshire. His mother was Anne Skinner and his father, Henry Wyatt, had been one of Henry VII's Privy Councillors, and remained a trusted adviser when Henry VIII came to the throne in 1509. In his turn, Thomas Wyatt followed his father to court after his education at St John's College, Cambridge. None of Wyatt's poems were published during his lifetime—the first book to feature his verse, *Tottel's Miscellany* of 1557, was printed a full fifteen years after his death.

Although hardly a household name today, Wyatt is an important figure in the history of English Literature. Wyatt's professed object was to experiment with the English tongue, to civilise it, to raise its powers to those of its neighbours. A significant amount of his literary output consists of translations and imitations of sonnets by the Italian poet Petrarch; he also wrote sonnets of his own. He took subject matter from Petrarch's sonnets, but his rhyme schemes make a significant departure. Petrarch's sonnets consist of an "octave", rhyming *abba abba*, followed, after a turn (volta) in the sense, by a "sestet" with various rhyme schemes. Wyatt employs the Petrarchan octave, but his most common sestet scheme is *cddc ee*. This marks the beginnings of an exclusively "English" contribution to sonnet structure, that is three quatrains and a closing couplet. Fifteen years after his death, the printer Richard Tottel included 97 poems attributed to Wyatt among the 271 poems in Tottel's Miscellany, *Songs and Sonnets*.

In addition to imitations of works by the classical writers Seneca and Horace, he experimented in stanza forms including the sonnet, the rondeau, epigrams, terza rima, ottava rima songs, satires and also with monorime, triplets with refrains, quatrains with different length of line and rhyme schemes, quatrains with codas, and the French forms of douzaine and treizaine. Wyatt introduced contemporaries to his *poulter's measure* form (Alexandrine couplets of twelve syllable iambic lines alternating with a fourteener, fourteen syllable line), and is acknowledged a master of the iambic tetrameter (an eight syllable line with four stresses).

While Wyatt's poetry reflects classical and Italian models, he also admired the work of Chaucer and his vocabulary reflects Chaucer's (for example, his use of Chaucer's word *newfangleness*, meaning fickle, in *They flee from me that sometime did me seek*). Many of his poems deal with the trials of romantic love, and the devotion of the suitor to an unavailable or cruel mistress. Others of his poems are scathing, satirical indictments of the hypocrisies and flat-out pandering required of courtiers ambitious to advance at the Tudor court.

Wyatt was one of the earliest poets of the English Renaissance. He was responsible for many innovations in English poetry and, alongside Henry Howard, Earl of Surrey, introduced the sonnet from Italy into England. His lyrics show tenderness of feeling and purity of diction. He is one of the originators of the convention in love poetry according to which the mistress is painted as hard-hearted and cruel, and therefore unattainable.

It is rumoured that Wyatt had a romantic liaison with Anne Boleyn before she attracted the attentions of the king, Henry VIII. Henry wooed Anne and she became his second wife – thus making her unattainable for Wyatt. This poem is about Anne Boleyn and how she is now out of reach, since Henry VIII is in love with her, and Wyatt's affair with her must come to an end.

Whoso – whoever

list – likes

hind – a female deer and a metaphor for Anne Boleyn

helas – 'Alas' in French; pronounced 'AYLA'

Draw – withdraw

afore – before

Sithens – since

Who list her hunt – who wishes to hunt her

graven – engraved

Noli me tangere – Latin for 'do not touch me'. Jesus says this to Mary Magdalene in St John's Gospel, Chapter 20, verse 17

Caesar's – Henry VIII's

Who? The poet speaks as himself, but not to a general reader. Only men went hunting in the 16th century generally, so we can argue that his audience is other men, more specifically the men of Henry VIII's court.

When? No specific time of day is mentioned; we know the poem was written in the early 16th century but was not published until after Wyatt's death. It is likely that a manuscript form of the poem was circulated among Wyatt's closest friends.

Where? No specific location. Hunting a deer may suggest a woodland setting, but we know that this is a poem about the pursuit of an individual woman – so if the setting is anywhere it is the king's court.

What? The poet warns other men not to 'hunt' a particular 'hind' because she belongs to the king. He has been exhausted and frustrated in his pursuit of her.

Commentary

This, one of the first sonnets ever to be written in English, uses an extended metaphor to describe the pursuit of a woman. The woman is described as a hind (a female deer) and the pursuit of her love and affection is compared to hunting a deer. This extended metaphor or conceit, it could be argued, puts the men in the poem firmly in charge of the conduct and progress of love, and implies that the women are weaker – but with a certain wild element, which arguably makes them all the more attractive and worthy of pursuit. It is generally accepted that this poem is specifically about Anne Boleyn who was vivacious, flirtatious and very attractive. She was a member of Henry VIII's court, and Wyatt and others were deeply attracted to her. However, the king himself was also attracted to Anne Boleyn and to get in the way of Henry and his desires was to invite death by execution.

It is interesting to speculate who the audience of this poem was: the poem was published after Wyatt's death, and it may have circulated in manuscript form among Wyatt's closest friends and intimate acquaintances. Certainly the poem seems addressed to other men in the royal court – and that makes it slightly untypical of the poems in the Anthology since most of the poems are addressed directly to a particular woman. The poem speaks of the poet's distress at his unrequited love and also warns other men that this particular woman is the property of the king.

The poem itself begins with a confidential tone, the speaker claiming that he knows where a female deer is for those interested in hunting

Whoso list to hunt, I know where is an hind.

However, in the second line he exclaims – *hélas, I may no more* – he can no longer participate in the hunt, because it has been a *vain travail* and it has *wearied [him] so sore* that he is the last in the hunt for this deer.

In the second quatrain a note of desperation creeps in as the poet admits that

…I by no means my wearied mind

Draw from the deer

and he persists in following her, despite the futility of the chase. He tries to rest and forget her but it is impossible – like trying to catch the wind in a net:

Fainting I follow, I leave off therefore,

Sithens in a net I seek to hold the wind.

In line 9 Wyatt uses a volta or turn to address other would-be hunters of this female deer. Wyatt is concerned to put other hunters out of doubt that to pursue this deer is a waste of time and dangerous because she wears a diamond necklace round her neck which reads

Noli me tangere, for Caesar's I am.

Anne Boleyn is the king's and, therefore, untouchable.

The final line of the sonnet sums up the risk of wooing Anne but also her attractiveness:

…wild for to hold, though I seem tame.

Her wildness hints at her attractive, lively personality as well as making clear the dangers of a liaison with her.

Like many of the poems in the Anthology this poem deals with unrequited love and presents it is deeply hurtful, frustrating and futile. Feminist critics will point out that this is a poem by a man –

written for an audience of men – and that the extended metaphor of a deer hunt, effectively reduces Anne Boleyn to the status of an animal. However, it might also be said that Wyatt has cleverly used a real pastime of the royal court – deer-hunting – to express his desire for Anne.

In this poem, one of the first sonnets in the English language, Wyatt:

- uses the extended metaphor of a deer hunt to describe his pursuit of a woman;
- expresses the pain he feels in such a futile pursuit;
- writes about real events concerning real people at the royal court;
- manages to express deep desire, while at the same time making it clear he is withdrawing from the pursuit of this particular woman.

Further reading: *Essential Poems* 978-1511935869

'Sonnet 116' – William Shakespeare

Let me not to the marriage of true minds
Admit impediments. Love is not love
Which alters when it alteration finds,
Or bends with the remover to remove:
O no; it is an ever-fixed mark,
That looks on tempests, and is never shaken;
It is the star to every wandering bark,
Whose worth's unknown, although his height be taken.
Love's not Time's fool, though rosy lips and cheeks
Within his bending sickle's compass come;
Love alters not with his brief hours and weeks,
But bears it out even to the edge of doom.
   If this be error and upon me proved,
   I never writ, nor no man ever loved.

Context

Shakespeare is the most famous writer England has ever produced and his plays are known throughout the world. 'Sonnet 116' by William Shakespeare is part of a sonnet sequence of 154 sonnets – also known as a sonnet cycle. Readers have commented that in the sonnets as a whole, Shakespeare covers every aspect of arguably the most important and strongest human emotion – love - as well as our most powerful instinct – sexual desire and the whole range of what happens in what we now call human relationships. Unlike Shakespeare's plays (most of which were unpublished during his lifetime), the sonnets were published in 1609. What does this tell us? We are not entirely sure: it is generally felt that it shows that poetry was held in higher regard than writing plays, so perhaps Shakespeare published the sonnets to achieve fame and wealth; there is also the fact that in Shakespeare's era there were no copyright laws – so once a play was published, there was nothing to stop any theatre putting a play on without giving the writer any performance fees.

 Of the 154 sonnets some are very famous and appear in many anthologies. These very famous ones are well-known by the general public too: in the past, BBC Radio 4 has sometimes run public surveys to discover the nation's favourite poem or the nation's favourite love poem and Shakespeare's sonnets are frequently voted into the top ten. If you like 'Sonnet 116', then you might like to read some of his others. They are readily available on-line and are known by their number and the first line:

Sonnet 18 – Shall I compare thee to a summer's day?

Sonnet 29 – When in disgrace with Fortune and men's eyes

Sonnet 55 – Not marble or the gilded monuments

Sonnet 57 – Being your slave what should I do?

Sonnet 71 – No longer mourn for me when I am dead

Sonnet 91 – Some glory in their birth, some in their skill

Sonnet 129 – The expense of spirit in a waste of shame

Sonnet 130 – My mistress' eyes are nothing like the sun

Because so little is known about Shakespeare's private life, there has been endless speculation about who the sonnets are addressed to –

but none of this speculation helps us get any closer to the individual sonnets and their meaning and impact. Personally I find it of no interest whatsoever, because for me the words are what make the sonnets memorable and worth reading now – over four hundred years since they were first published.

'Sonnet 116' is often used in modern marriage services (nowadays some churches allow couples considerable freedom in choosing some of the words they use during the service) and I have even seen cards for sale which reproduce the words of the sonnet – these cards are intended to be sent to people who are getting married. The whole sonnet presents a love that is steadfast and loyal and unchanging in the face of other changes. We will look closely at the language and tone of the sonnet, but also consider a deeper and darker interpretation.

impediments – obstacles.

or…remove – or ends when one person leaves or stops the relationship.

ever-fixèd – permanent, not moving.

bark – ship.

time's fool – the fool of time, subject to time and ageing.

bending sickle – a scythe and its curved shape; the Grim Reaper carries a sickle; sickles and scythes are long-handled tools used for chopping down tall crops or weeds; here it is used metaphorically – Time chops us down because we succumb to age and finally death.

compass – range.

bears it out – endures it.

doom – Doomsday, the end of the world in Christian mythology, the day of Final Judgement when Christ will come to earth again and decide who goes to Heaven and who to Hell. Shakespeare uses this to suggest that love will last forever – until the end of time or the end of the world.

Who? The voice of the poet – but the commentary that follows suggests the implied presence of other people.

When? The sonnets were published in 1609, but most scholars believe that Shakespeare began to write them in the 1590s. Within the poem no particular time is specified.

Where? No particular place is specified, so the location does not seem important.

What? Shakespeare states that true love will never change and then explores this assertion through a series of images in order to prove or demonstrate that true love will never alter no matter what.

Commentary

The opening sentence of the sonnet is justly famous: the recurrence of the letter *m* which both alliterates and is within certain words and the way the first line runs on into the second

Let me not to the marriage of true minds

Admit impediments

creates a gentle, calm, mellifluous tone which is appropriate to the sense: assonance on the letter *l* creates euphony, which is all enhanced by the enjambment. The next sentence too

Love is not love

Which alters when it alteration finds.

is often quoted on its own and offered as a universal truth: true love never changes no matter what happens. This second sentence is memorable not just because of the sentiment but because of the words: the repetition of the word *love* as well as *alter/alteration* and the soft sounds of the letter *l* and *w* and *f*. So far the sonnet is quite clearly concerned with marriage and *alters* is a pun on what we find at the eastern end of a church - the altar. *Impediment* too is a word, a very important word, in the Church of England marriage service. In the marriage service the priest says to the congregation, before the couple exchange their vows of marriage:

Does anyone know of any just cause or impediment why these two should not be joined together in holy matrimony?

Impediment here means an obstacle. At this point in the service, centuries ago, this was the moment when someone in the congregation could mention an obstacle – such as one of the couple being already married or promised to someone else or below the legal age to marry or whatever. The final line of the quatrain continues this pattern of repetition – *remover/remove.*

The second quatrain introduces new images in an effort to define what love is. Line 5 begins with a dramatic exclamation – *O no* – and then introduces a metaphor based on ships and navigation. Love is *ever-fixèd*: it never changes and can endure the fury of tempests without being shaken; love is like a star that guides sailors who would otherwise be lost (*wandering*) and they measure the height of the star (love) even before they understand whether the star will help them navigate. Shakespeare uses assonance – *star* assonates with the rhyme words *bark* and *mark* – and *whose worth's unknown* – repeats the same sound with *o* – which also goes back to the exclamation at the start of the quatrain. This creates a sort of aural harmony even though he is writing about potentially dangerous things – tempests, and ships that are lost.

The third quatrain changes the line of thought again. It starts with a bold statement – *Love's not Time's fool*; Shakespeare means that true love will not alter even though time changes our physical appearance as we age. Time destroys *rosy lips and cheeks*. Note the consonance on *c* in *sickle's compass come*. Line 11 deliberately echoes the opening quatrain with its use of *alters*. The whole quatrain is held together not just by sense and subject matter and rhyme, but also alliteration – *bending, brief, but bears*. The final line says that love will last until Doomsday, the end of time.

The sonnet ends with an assertive couplet. Shakespeare states that if he is wrong – that if love is impermanent or transitory then it follows that he, the poet, never wrote a word and no human being ever really loved.

This poem is usually read as a definition of love or true love: an emotion that survives time and tempests, that will never change, no matter what happens. This is why it is so popular in connection with marriages – it serves, people think, as a vow of love that will last forever. Perhaps its power has a lot to do with its sounds: we have noted the clever use of repetition; the euphony created by the soft consonants in the opening quatrain; and, perhaps, its appeal has something to do with Shakespeare's straightforward imagery of stars and ships, rosy cheeks, death personified with his bending sickle. However, a closer reading will show that there is another possibility, another way to interpret this very famous poem.

Remember that in the first sentence Shakespeare had said he was not going to admit impediments – he is going to say nothing at this point of the marriage service. This suggests that Shakespeare is writing about the marriage of someone else and asserting that he still loves that person and his love will never change, despite the fact that they are marrying someone else and not him. It is ironic, isn't it, that the sonnet is so often used in marriage services: this is a poem about the end of a relationship – a relationship that is ending because one of the people involved in the relationship is getting married. Consequently, the speaker's feelings are of sadness and a sense of betrayal, but they are controlled by the strict form of the sonnet which helps to restrain the terrible sadness the speaker feels.

In the light of this reading of the poem, the poem's imagery still fits with what I wrote earlier in the summary, but some of the images take on a darker, sadder tone and atmosphere. The simile involving the *wandering bark* works as a simile, but it might also suggest Shakespeare's emotional state now that his former lover has rejected him to marry someone else – he is like a ship drifting. Love that bears it out until the edge of doom, means a love that will never die and will keep going until Doomsday, but that word *doom* perhaps suggests the terrible sadness that Shakespeare feels at the end of the relationship: in a sense it is almost like the end of the world for him. *Bears it out* suggests a determination to keep going despite the heartbreak he feels – and he does, in a sense, keep going, because the sonnet reaches its conclusion.

Why?

This world-famous poem

- offers a definition of love which many readers have found comforting and inspiring.

- asserts that true love lasts forever and will endure absence and time and even death.

- uses simple repetition and wonderfully crafted combinations of sound to create euphony.

BUT it might also be read as

- a poem full of heartbreak and sadness at the loss of a loved one who marries someone else.

Further reading: *The Complete Sonnets* ISBN: 978-1497343207

The Flea – John Donne

Mark but this flea, and mark in this,
How little that which thou deniest me is;
It sucked me first, and now sucks thee,
And in this flea our two bloods mingled be;
Thou know'st that this cannot be said
A sin, nor shame, nor loss of maidenhead,
   Yet this enjoys before it woo,
   And pampered swells with one blood made of two,
   And this, alas, is more than we would do.

Oh stay, three lives in one flea spare,
Where we almost, nay more than married are.
This flea is you and I, and this
Our mariage bed, and marriage temple is;
Though parents grudge, and you, w'are met,
And cloistered in these living walls of jet.
   Though use make you apt to kill me,
   Let not to that, self-murder added be,
   And sacrilege, three sins in killing three.

Cruel and sudden, hast thou since
Purpled thy nail, in blood of innocence?
Wherein could this flea guilty be,
Except in that drop which it sucked from thee?
Yet thou triumph'st, and say'st that thou
Find'st not thy self, nor me the weaker now;
   'Tis true; then learn how false, fears be:
   Just so much honor, when thou yield'st to me,
   Will waste, as this flea's death took life from thee.

Author & Context

John Donne was born on January 22, 1572, in London, England. He is known as the founder of the Metaphysical Poets, a term created by Samuel Johnson, an eighteenth-century English essayist, poet, and philosopher. The loosely associated group also includes George Herbert, Richard Crashaw, Andrew Marvell, and John Cleveland. The Metaphysical Poets are known for their ability to startle the reader and coax new perspective through paradoxical images, subtle argument, inventive syntax, and imagery from art, philosophy, and religion using an extended metaphor known as a conceit. Donne reached beyond the rational and hierarchical structures of the seventeenth century with his exacting and ingenious conceits, advancing the exploratory spirit of his time.

Donne entered the world during a period of theological and political unrest for both England and France; a Protestant massacre occurred on Saint Bartholomew's day in France; while in England, the Catholics were the persecuted minority. Born into a Roman Catholic family, Donne's personal relationship with religion was tumultuous and passionate, and at the centre of much of his poetry. He studied at both Oxford and Cambridge Universities in his early teen years.

He did not take a degree at either school, because to do so would have meant subscribing to the Thirty-nine Articles, the doctrine that defined Anglicanism. At age twenty he studied law at Lincoln's Inn. Two years later he succumbed to religious pressure and joined the Anglican Church after his younger brother, convicted for his Catholic loyalties, died in prison. Donne wrote most of his love lyrics, erotic verse, and some sacred poems in the 1590s, creating two major volumes of work: *Satires* and *Songs and Sonnets*.

In 1598, after returning from a two-year naval expedition against Spain, Donne was appointed private secretary to Sir Thomas Egerton. While sitting in Queen Elizabeth's last Parliament in 1601, Donne secretly married Anne More, the sixteen-year-old niece of Lady Egerton. Donne's father-in-law disapproved of the marriage. As punishment, he did not provide a dowry for the couple and had Donne briefly imprisoned.

This left the couple isolated and dependent on friends, relatives, and patrons. Donne suffered social and financial instability in the years following his marriage, exacerbated by the birth of many children. He continued to write and published the *Divine Poems* in 1607. In *Pseudo-Martyr*, published in 1610, Donne displayed his extensive knowledge of the laws of the Church and state, arguing that Roman Catholics could support James I without compromising their faith. In 1615, James I pressured him to enter the Anglican Ministry by declaring that Donne could not be employed outside of the Church. He was appointed Royal Chaplain later that year. His wife died in 1617 at thirty-three years old shortly after giving birth to their twelfth child, who was stillborn. The *Holy Sonnets* are also attributed to this phase of his life.

In 1621, he became dean of Saint Paul's Cathedral. In his later years, Donne's writing reflected his fear of his inevitable death. He wrote his private prayers, *Devotions upon Emergent Occasions*, during a period of severe illness and published them in 1624. His learned, charismatic, and inventive preaching made him a highly influential presence in London. Best known for his vivacious, compelling style and thorough examination of mortal paradox, John Donne died in London on March 31, 1631.

Mark but this flea – just look at this flea.

maidenhead – virginity.

Who? The poet addresses his lover.

When? No specific time.

Where? No specific location – but the lovers must be in a relaxed informal setting, perhaps in bed, certainly alone.

What? The poem revolves around a flea. In the first stanza it has sucked blood from both the poet and his lover. In the second stanza Donne pleads with his lover not to kill the flea. Between the second and third stanza the poet's lover squashes the flea with her nail – but Donne uses this fact to further and to strengthen his argument.

Commentary

'The Flea' is a complex poem of seduction and argument. It has a lot in common with 'To His Coy Mistress' by Andrew Marvell which also contains an argument and is also a Metaphysical poem. The metaphysical poets is a term coined by the poet and critic

Samuel Johnson to describe a loose group of English lyric poets of the 17th century, whose work was characterized by the inventive use of conceits, and by speculation about topics such as love or religion. Their work is also characterized by complex and intriguing arguments. In 'The Flea' Donne's originality lies not simply is his argument, but also in his choice of a flea to symbolize the love between the him and the woman he addresses: it is hard to think of an insect more loathed than a flea... but Donne wittily and cleverly bases his whole argument of seduction around this much-loathed insect and – in so doing – adds a level of sardonic humour to his poem. Is the flea the most despised insect in all of creation? Donne's originality is that he turns the flea into a symbol – light-hearted enough – of the love, the physical love, between him and his lover!

Sex involves the mingling of blood (especially when the woman's virginity is taken) and it is this notion which informs Donne's argument. In the first two lines he invites his lover to

Mark but this flea, and mark in this,

How little that which thou deniest me is.

The flea has sucked blood from Donne and from his lover 'And in this flea our two bloods mingled be'. The mingling of their blood in the flea

...cannot be said

A sin, nor shame, nor loss of maidenhead

But the flea 'enjoys before it woo'

And pampered swells with one blood made of two,

And this, alas, is more than we would do.

Donne is trying to persuade his lover to have sex with him and 'swells' – although it refers to the flea filled with the blood of both of them – also suggests the swelling of the male penis during sex.

In the second stanza his lover is about to squash the flea but Donne implores her to 'stay' and spare 'three lives' in one flea – three lives because there is the life of the flea and the blood of the two lovers which the flea is full of. Then, through a remarkable leap of the imagination, Donne claims that, because it contains the blood of both of them

This flea is you and I, and this

Our marriage bed, and marriage temple is

despite the objections of her and her parents ('Though parents grudge, and you').

Donne's witty intelligence shines out at the end of the second stanza: having established – purely through words and argument that the flea contains his blood and her blood and (he says) is their 'marriage temple', he urges her not to squash the flea because in doing so she will kill him and her (self-murder) and sacrilege – the destruction of their marriage temple. We also have the line

Though use make you apt to kill me.

'Kill' is a metaphor suggesting she mistreats him by denying him her love and by refusing to sleep with him.

Between the second and third stanza his lover kills the flea with her nail (which is 'purpled' with the flea) and which leads Donne to berate her for being 'Cruel and sudden' and arguing that the flea only deserved to die because it has sucked her blood. Seamlessly Donne moves to the final part of his argument. His lover – having killed the flea – finds herself and Donne no weaker than before:

Yet thou triumphest, and say'st that thou

Find'st not thy self, nor me the weaker now.

It follows, therefore, that if the death of the flea leaves both lovers strong (despite it containing his blood and her blood and being their marriage temple), then Donne's making love to her will be a similarly trivial thing.

And Donne turns this to his advantage in his finale, his final argument: if the killing of the flea is such a trivial thing then it follows that when his lover gives herself to him she has nothing to fear:

'Tis true; then learn how false fears be:

Just so much honour, when thou yield'st to me.

Through his convoluted and amusing sophistry, Donne attempts to convince his lover that she will lose as much honour by making love to him as the flea lost in being killed i.e. not very much! This is a witty and persuasive poem, full of sexual innuendo and with a light-hearted and playful tone.

Why?

In 'The Flea' Donne

- wittily and with light-hearted good humour uses the extended conceit of a flea as part of an argument to persuade his lover to sleep with him;
- writes a complex and clever argument;
- flatters his lover by the complexity of his argument;
- writes a poem full of sexual innuendo;
- entertains the reader with the twists and turns of his argument.

Further reading: *Songs and Sonets* ISBN: 978-1505855523

'To His Coy Mistress' – Andrew Marvell

Had we but world enough and time,
This coyness, lady, were no crime.
We would sit down, and think which way
To walk, and pass our long love's day.
Thou by the Indian Ganges' side
Shouldst rubies find; I by the tide
Of Humber would complain. I would
Love you ten years before the flood,
And you should, if you please, refuse
Till the conversion of the Jews.
My vegetable love should grow
Vaster than empires and more slow;
An hundred years should go to praise
Thine eyes, and on thy forehead gaze;
Two hundred to adore each breast,
But thirty thousand to the rest;
An age at least to every part,
And the last age should show your heart.
For, lady, you deserve this state,
Nor would I love at lower rate.
     But at my back I always hear
Time's wingèd chariot hurrying near;
And yonder all before us lie
Deserts of vast eternity.
Thy beauty shall no more be found;
Nor, in thy marble vault, shall sound
My echoing song; then worms shall try
That long-preserved virginity,
And your quaint honour turn to dust,
And into ashes all my lust;

The grave's a fine and private place,
But none, I think, do there embrace.
  Now therefore, while the youthful glew
Sits on thy skin like morning dew,
And while thy willing soul transpires
At every pore with instant fires,
Now let us sport us while we may,
And now, like amorous birds of prey,
Rather at once our time devour
Than languish in his slow-chapped power.
Let us roll all our strength and all
Our sweetness up into one ball,
And tear our pleasures with rough strife
Through the iron gates of life:
Thus, though we cannot make our sun
Stand still, yet we will make him run.

Context & Author

Andrew Marvell was born in a village near Hull in 1621. His father was a Church of England vicar. Marvell went to Cambridge where he wrote some of his first poems in Latin and Greek and it is believed he then travelled widely in Europe. The 1640s were turbulent and violent years in the history of England. A destructive Civil War between Parliament and the King was fought out with the King's forces finally being defeated in 1645 at the Battle of Naseby. Charles I was eventually put on trial, found guilty of treason and executed by parliament on January 29th 1649: England became a republic.

Marvell was closely associated with the Parliamentary side: in the late

1640s he was employed as tutor to Mary Fairfax, the daughter of Sir Thomas Fairfax, Commander in Chief of the parliamentary army and then in the 1650s he worked in Cromwell's government. In 1659 he became MP for Hull and remained as MP until his death in 1678. He was a hard-working MP and stood up for freedom of speech and religious toleration, when these came under threat from Charles II, who had returned to England in 1660 to take the crown and restore the monarchy. His published poems in this period (known as the Restoration) were bitterly satirical about the corruption he saw in the royal court, and some were published anonymously so that he did not get into trouble with the authorities. 'To His Coy Mistress' and about another 80 poems were published posthumously: we are not sure when they were written but there is general agreement that they were probably written in the late 1640s when Marvell worked for Fairfax at his estate in Yorkshire.

Coy – bashful or shy in an affected way.

Mistress – lover. The word in the 17th century did not have its modern connotations of a woman other than a man's wife.

Had we – if we had.

World – space.

Ganges – sacred river in India; only a handful of Englishmen would have actually seen the Ganges when Marvell wrote this poem.

Humber – a river in the north of England which reaches the sea near Hull – near where Marvell was born.

The Flood – he is referring to the story of the Flood in the Bible which took place thousands of years ago.

The conversion of the Jews – an indirect allusion to the Day of Judgment – which may be thousands of years away; according to Christian belief, on the Day of Judgment all Jews will realize they were wrong and be converted to Christianity.

quaint – a pun. It means prim and proper, but was also a 17th century alternative spelling of 'cunt'.

dust – an allusion to the Church of England funeral service – ashes to ashes, dust to dust.

glew – glue, sweat, perspiration.

sport us – enjoy ourselves.

slow-chapt – slowly chewed.

Who? The poem is written in the first person and addressed to Marvell's mistress. It starts in the future conditional tense (*I would love you...*) and then changes to the present in the second and third verse paragraphs.

When? The present. The poem is generally thought to been written around 1649, when Marvell was tutor to Maria Fairfax. Her father, Sir Thomas Fairfax, had been Commander in Chief of the Parliamentary Army in the Civil War against the king.

Where? Specific places are mentioned, but the poem itself has no particular setting.

What? Marvell uses the first verse paragraph to describe how he would love his mistress if they had all the time in the world; he then points out that death is inevitable; in the third and final verse paragraph he urges her to make love with him now.

Commentary

'Carpe diem' is a Latin phrase which means 'Seize the day'; in other words, live life to the full now, because life is short and tomorrow we may be dead. It was a very common theme for poets to write about in the 16th and 17th centuries, perhaps because life and death were more unpredictable, life expectancy was shorter and medical knowledge very primitive. It is also possible to relate the idea to the Civil War: in times of warfare you may feel even more at risk and that life is precarious and death just that little bit closer. We do not place much emphasis in schools on the English Civil War, but some historians have calculated that it was the bloodiest civil war ever: not in terms of the total number of deaths, but in terms of the number of deaths as a proportion of the population. So for those who lived through it, it must have been a traumatic, disturbing event. All the more reason then, to seize the day.

Another notable feature of this poem is its syllogistic structure: it is a carefully constructed argument. The first verse paragraph presents one possible scenario; the second proves it cannot happen like that: the third verse paragraph reaches a conclusion. This sort of logical progression is very typical of Metaphysical poetry.

The opening verse paragraph is full of hyperbole. Marvell tells his mistress how he would love her, if they had enough space and time. The rhythm is slow and sensual. If they had all the time in the world then they could sit and think how to

...pass our long love's day.

Note how those three words at the end of the line are all stressed and the way *long* and *love* alliterate and assonate. Even physical separation would not be a problem: the poet could be complaining on the banks of the Humber, while his lover could be finding rubies by the side of the Ganges. What would he be complaining about? Well, the fact that they are apart. I find this image very funny because it juxtaposes the very exotic (Ganges and rubies) with the very ordinary English river – the Humber. Marvell then uses hyperbole to suggest how long he would love her: from thousands of years ago (the Biblical Flood) to thousands of years in the future (Doomsday). The next couplet is wonderfully suggestive in its imagery

My vegetable love should grow

Vaster than empires, and more slow.

The poet seems to be boasting that if he loved her for that length of time his erection would become enormous. He then tells her how long he would praise and adore her: two hundred years

... to adore each breast.

This is richly comic hyperbole – foreplay that would last for several millennia.

The second verse paragraph begins with the word *but* and Marvell reveals why they cannot spend so long building up to sex – because they will die. He says he is always aware of

Time's winged chariot hurrying near.

What awaits them are

Deserts of vast eternity.

Death will destroy her beauty and his *echoing song* (his poetry). The poet then gives a detailed picture of what will happen to her body when she is dead:

...then worms shall try

That long-preserved virginity,

And your quaint honour turn to dust.

This is a gruesome image – the worms burrowing into his mistress's vagina instead of him burrowing into her. The phrase *quaint honour* could be argued to be the rudest, funniest pun in the whole of English poetry. Marvell is saying that her honour is old-fashioned and silly, but also it is honour to do with her quaint – her cunt. I find this hilarious and deliberately shocking. The word *dust* (from the funeral service) deliberately rhymes with *lust* to underline the fact that they must seize the moment. The verse paragraph ends with this couplet:

The grave's a fine and private place

But none, I think, do there embrace.

Of course, the idea of two skeletons embracing each other in the grave is gruesome and impossible, but what makes me laugh in this couplet is Marvell's *I think* – as though there were any doubt whatsoever about it!!

The final verse paragraph begins with the word *Now* – and Marvell reaches his conclusion: because they are going to die, they must make love immediately. The word *now* is repeated twice more before the end of the poem – an indication of the poet's urgency and impatience. The word *therefore* reminds us that this is an argument. Marvell wants to make love while his mistress is still young: while the *youthful hue* colours her skin and while she is full of *instant fires* and capable of passion. The imagery Marvell uses to describe their love-making is full of oxymoron: the simile *like amorous birds of prey* is especially striking. *Amorous* means loving, but birds of prey tear the flesh from other creatures – this is love which is energetic, loving, but also wild and rough. He imagines that they will devour time rather than be slowly chewed up by time itself. This imagines time as a monster who chews us up by ageing us and eventually killing us. Lines 41 and 42 are especially interesting:

Let us roll all our strength and all

Our sweetness up into one ball.

Try reading this aloud. The mainly monosyllabic words and the words beginning with vowels and ending in *l* are difficult to enunciate without slurring the words together – to say them properly makes you slow down and also takes some effort – but then he is describing the sexual act which also takes some effort. As for the ball – some readers suggest this a cannon-ball and make much of the fact that Marvell lived through the Civil War; others suggest it is a sexual position. I am undecided. It is probably both.

As the poem proceeds the act of love is seen as pleasurable but also painful in an enjoyable way. He promises her that they will

… tear our pleasures with rough strife

Through the iron gates of life.

The word *pleasures* is juxtaposed with *tear* and *rough strife* – an act of love which gives pleasure and pain. The *gates of life* are the entrance to his lover's vagina.

The final couplet means that by having sex, they will not be able to make time (here symbolized by the sun) stop (*stand still*) but they will make time go quickly (*run*). It also begins with *thus* and presents the final conclusion to the poet's argument.

The rhythm of this poem is particularly effective. To put it briefly, it mirrors what it describes: the first verse paragraph is slow and leisurely; the second starts to speed up; and the final verse paragraph is very quick. Why? It is partly because the situation is urgent and pressing – they might die at any moment. Marvell is in a hurry and the rhythm of the poem reflects this. The rhythm also mirrors the sexual act to reach a climax in the final couplet: sex starts slowly and then gets quicker and quicker.

How does Marvell achieve this speeding up of the rhythm in the final third of the poem? And how does he create the slow rhythm of the opening section? The first verse paragraph has a lot of sentences or uses colons to create heavy pauses; there is some enjambment but there are heavy caesuras which then slow the poem down. By contrast, the third verse paragraph consists of only three sentences, there are very few caesuras and extensive use of enjambment – so when it is read aloud it has to be read more quickly and the words are largely monosyllabic so that there is a pounding, regular rhythm – like that of the sexual act.

Let's look in detail at the final couplet:

Thus, though we cannot make our sun

Stand still, yet we will make him run.

The first line flows into the second through enjambment; alliteration then foregrounds *sun stands still* which is followed by perhaps the best-placed caesura in English poetry – if you read it aloud your voice has to stop and stand still so it reflects the sense superbly. Also, given what Marvell is writing` about here – the sexual act – it is not hard to see that pause in the line as the moment of climax. You may feel I am reading too much into one comma, BUT this is a poem that has boasted of his vegetable love, imagined worms burrowing into his lover's vagina and punned on the word *quaint* – so it is more than likely that Marvell places that comma and the alliteration and enjambment that precede it with precise care.

The poem is written in iambic tetrameters (8 syllables, four stresses) but Marvell uses a lot of metrical variation to enhance the meaning of the words. For example, *long day* is a spondee (which along with the alliteration on *love's*) lengthens the sounds to give us an impression of the length of the day. *Vaster* starts the line with a trochee – as if to emphasize the sheer vastness of Marvell's vegetable love. *Deserts* is a trochee – starting the line with a forceful sound. As I have implied above *Stand still* in the final line is a spondee which (with the caesura) brings the sense to an abrupt and arresting stop, a moment of climax in a poem about sex. It is worth scanning some of the final lines to see the preponderance of stressed syllables which contribute to the strong, pounding rhythm (and try reading them aloud):

Let us **roll all** our **strength** and **all**
Our **sweet**ness **up** into **one ball**,
And **tear** our **plea**sures with **rough strife**
Through the **ir**on **gates** of **life**:
Thus, though we **can**not **make our sun**
Stand still, yet we will **make him run**.

Clearly here the pounding, insistent rhythm of the lines is designed to imitate the rhythms of sex, and Marvell at times allows five stressed syllables in the line to reflect the urgent rhythm more clearly.

Why?

This very famous and much-anthologized poem

- presents the inevitability of death in frightening images;

- celebrates the physicality of sex;

- uses outrageous humour and frankness to write originally on a stereotypical theme (carpe diem);

- matches its rhythm perfectly to its subject matter;

- manages to be very funny and very serious at the same time;

- is probably the greatest carpe diem poem in the English language.

Further reading: *The Complete Lyric Poetry* ISBN: 978-1480075146

'The Scrutiny' – Richard Lovelace

Why should you sweare I am forsworn,
   Since thine I vow'd to be?
Lady it is already Morn,
   And 'twas last night I swore to thee
That fond impossibility.

II

Have I not lov'd thee much and long,
   A tedious twelve houres space?
I must all other Beauties wrong,
   And rob thee of a new imbrace;
Could I still dote upon thy Face.

III

Not, but all joy in thy browne haire,
   By others may be found;
But I must search the blank and faire
   Like skilful Minerallist's that sound
For Treasure in un-plow'd-up ground.

IV

Then, if when I have lov'd my round,
   Thou prov'st the pleasant she;
With spoyles of meaner Beauties crown'd,
   I laden will returne to thee,
Ev'd sated with Varietie.

Context & Author

Richard Lovelace (1617–1657) was an English poet in the seventeenth century. He was a cavalier poet who fought on behalf of the king during the Civil War. His best known works are "To Althea, from Prison," and "To Lucasta, Going to the Warres." Lovelace was sympathetic to the Royalist cause during the English Civil War and he was imprisoned by the parliamentary regime on several different occasions. As a Cavalier poet he owed his poetic influence to Ben Jonson's poetry rather than to the Metaphysical poets such as John Donne; indeed, the Cavalier poets were often referred to as the Sons of Ben or the Tribe of Ben. As a poem this is much less challenging than John Donne's 'The Flea' in terms of its argument, and does not contain anything like Donne's tortuous argument or something as original as a flea to put in a supposed love poem.

scrutiny – a careful and thorough investigation or examination.

forsworn – to have sworn falsely.

Minerallist's – one who searches for precious metals in the ground.

sated – satisfied

Who? The poet addresses his lover with whom he has spent the night.

When? The morning after a night of love-making.

Where? In bed.

What? Although they have spent twelve hours in bed together, Lovelace claims he is not hers alone and that he must make a 'scrutiny' of many other women before he can decide which is the right one for him – and, as he says at the end of the poem, it may be that he will return to her arms – but only after sleeping with many other women. His lover is given no voice in this poem.

Commentary

Many readers would see this as a selfish, self-centred poem. In the first stanza Lovelace reveals that he has spent the night with the woman he is addressing in the poem. At the beginning of their love-making he 'vow'd' to be hers, but now it is morning and he calls that a 'fond impossiblity'.

The second stanza begins

Have I not loved thee much and long,
A tedious twelve houres space?

The key word here is 'tedious' – the speaker has loved her throughout the night and now making love to her would be 'tedious'. By a remarkable feat of sophistry the speaker goes on to claim that he would 'wrong' 'all other beauties' if he were to remain faithful to her. He claims that making love to other women will allow him to return to her with a 'new embrace'.

The third stanza suggests that she too (the addressee of the poem) is free, like the speaker, to love other people:

...but all joy in thy browne haire,
By others may be found

Meanwhile, the speaker 'must search the blank and faire' – try out other women according to their hair colour

Like skillfull Mineralists that sound
For Treasure in un-plow'd-up ground.

Lovelace clearly extols the attractiveness and sexuality of women by use of the word 'treasure' – even if it is in a simile, comparing him to a collector of precious stones. 'Un-plowed-up ground' suggests very forcefully that the women Lovelace has in mind are virgins.

In the final stanza Lovelace claims that when he has 'lov'd my round' he will return to the addressee of the poem if

Thou prov'st the pleasanter she.

The speaker claims he will return with 'spoyles of meaner Beauties crown'd' and 'sated with Varietie'.

There is a sense in which this is a selfish, almost misogynistic poem: Lovelace is giving himself licence to sleep with many women. But there is more to it than that. In the third stanza the speaker gives the woman licence to sleep with other men and am I wrong to see a world-weary tone in the last two lines?

I laden will returne to thee
Ev'n sated with Varietie –

which suggests that 'Varietie' is not as fulfilling as we might think.

We must also consider the context: the English Civil War. In times of war, relationships are likely to be broken and problematic and possibly short-lived. The title 'The Scrutinie', at first glance, suggests the exhaustive scrutiny of other women that Lovelace proposes in the second stanza, but on deeper reflection the title could be seen as ironic and referring to the speaker and his casual, promiscuous and careless attitude to women (in other words a scrutiny of his morality). In this reading, the poem becomes a scrutiny of male promiscuity, arrogance and selfishness through egotistical gratification.

Why?

In this short poem, Lovelace

- praises by implication the physical delights of love;
- advocates promiscuity;
- shows little, if any, emotion towards his lover;
- reveals his feelings to be shallow, superficial and full of a solipsistic arrogance.

'Absent from Thee' - John Wilmot, Earl of Rochester

Absent from thee I languish still,
  Then ask me not, When I return?
The straying fool 'twill plainly kill
  To wish all day, all night to mourn.

Dear, from thine arms then let me fly,
  That my fantastic mind may prove
The torments it deserves to try,
  That tears my fix'd heart from my love.

When, wearied with a world of woe,
  To thy safe bosom I retire,
Where love, and peace, and truth does flow,
  May I, contented, there expire.

Lest once more wandering from that heaven,
  I fall on some base heart unblest,
Faithless to thee, false, unforgiven,
  And lose my everlasting rest.

Context and Author

John Wilmot, 2nd Earl of Rochester (1 April 1647 – 26 July 1680),
was an infamous English poet and courtier of King Charles
II's Restoration court. The Restoration reacted against the "spiritual
authoritarianism" of the Puritan era. Rochester was the embodiment
of the new era, and he is as well known for his promiscuous lifestyle
as his poetry, although the two were often interlinked. He died at
the age of 33 from venereal disease.

Although much of Rochester's verse is sexually overt (complete with taboo language), he was able to write touching and intimate poems such as 'Absent from Thee', which are tender and intimate in their tone and which ring with a psychological truth.

languish – to become depressed.

fantastic – capable of indulging in fantasy.

prove – experience.

torments – torture, painful anguish.

Who? The poet addresses his lover from whom he is absent.

When? No specific time.

Where? No specific location.

What? The speaker (almost certainly Rochester himself) can only find peace and rest when he is with his lover, and he is unhappy and forlorn when they are apart.

Commentary

Many of Rochester's poems are quite like the Lovelace poem above in their attitude to sex and to women, but 'Absent from thee I languish still' is a poem full of heart-felt tenderness, love and fidelity. It is a poem of parting and Rochester asserts that he will 'languish' while they are parted and begs his lover not to ask him when he will return because

The straying fool [Rochester himself] 'twill plainly kill

To wish all day, all night to mourn –

which clearly suggests he will spend all day wishing they were together and spend all night mourning that they are apart. It will not kill him – that is hyperbole – but the effects will be as bad as death he claims.

The second stanza begins with a plea to let him go in order that his mind may withstand the torments of being away from her and which 'tears my fixed heart from my love'.

In the third stanza he expresses the desire to return to her after his absence – 'when wearied with a world of woe' (re-inforced by the melancholy alliteration on 'w') and to retire to her 'safe bosom' which he associates with 'love, and peace, and truth' and where he 'contented...[may] expire.

The final stanza outlines the possibility of infidelity. Rochester describes his lover as 'heaven' and 'my everlasting rest', but is wary of falling 'on some base heart unblest' (another woman) and becoming 'Faithless to thee, false, unforgiven' and, as a result of hid infidelity, in a line which exudes religious overtones, 'lose my everlasting rest.'

This poem is almost contemporary with the poem by Lovelace above, but its sentiments are completely at odds with the earlier poem, investing a religious significance into Rochester's love for his unnamed lover. The poem is written in strict iambic tetrameters with an occasional line starting with a trochaic foot to draw attention to particular words and to provide metrical variation: 'Absent', 'Dear', 'May' and 'Faithless'.

The woman in this poem has no voice and is seen as a source of comfort and a sanctuary from 'a world of woe', but she is not treated with the flippant selfishness that Lovelace achieves. Instead Rochester's tone is loving and tender and implies fidelity to his lover.

This short lyric poem:

- expresses sincere love and desire for the poet's lover;
- presents his life as incomplete without her presence;
- presents being away from her as a 'world of woe';
- presents his love in religious terms as his 'heaven' and other women as 'unblest';
- is unequivocal in his love for his lover.

Further reading: *A Selection of Poetry* 978-1511609449

'The Garden of Love' – William Blake

I went to the Garden of Love,
And saw what I never had seen:
A Chapel was built in the midst,
Where I used to play on the green.

And the gates of this Chapel were shut,
And 'Thou shalt not' writ over the door;
So I turn'd to the Garden of Love,
That so many sweet flowers bore.

And I saw it was filled with graves,
And tomb-stones where flowers should be:
And Priests in black gowns, were walking their rounds,
And binding with briars, my joys & desires.

Context and Author

William Blake (1757 – 1827) is now seen as the foremost artist and poet of his time, but his work was largely unknown during his lifetime. He was a painter as well as a poet and you can see some of his paintings in art galleries like Tate Britain in London or the Fitzwilliam Museum in Cambridge. 'The Garden of Love' comes from the collection *Songs of Innocence and of Experience* which appeared together for the first time in 1794. *The Songs of Innocence* (which originally appeared on their own in 1789) are positive in tone and celebrate unspoilt nature, childhood and love. *The Songs of Experience* (from which 'The Garden of Love comes) depicts a corrupt society in which the prevailing mood is one of despair and in which children are exploited and love is corrupted.

Thou Shalt Not – a clear reminder of the Decalogue (the Ten Commandments) from the Old Testament. Of the Ten Commandments, eight of them contain the words 'thou shalt not' – which is why Blake disliked their repressive negativity. They are mainly about things you are not allowed to do – not what you can do

priest – an extremely provocative and pejorative word for Blake – it summed up for him all that was rigid and repressive about organized religion and the Church.

briars – bushes with hard, large and sharp thorns – used to beat people with.

Who? The speaker visits one of his childhood haunts to find it completely changed.

When? No specific time.

Where? In what was 'The Garden of Love', but which now has been transformed into a cemetery, ruled over by repressive priests.

What? The speaker of the poem returns to a green where he used to play as a child to find that it has been transformed by the Church into a cemetery with a chapel built in the middle.

In *Songs of Innocence and of Experience* the poems are generally paired, so a *Song of Experience* has its counterpart in *Innocence*. This is 'The Echoing Green' the counterpart from *Innocence* to 'The Garden of Love':

The sun does arise,
And make happy the
skies.
The merry bells ring
To welcome the Spring.
The sky-lark and
thrush,
The birds of the bush,
Sing louder around,
To the bells' cheerful
sound.
While our sports shall
be seen
On the Ecchoing
Green.

Old John, with white
hair
Does laugh away care,
Sitting under the oak,
Among the old folk,

They laugh at our play,
And soon they all say.
'Such, such were the joys.
When we all girls & boys,
In our youth-time were seen,
On the Ecchoing Green.'

Till the little ones weary
No more can be merry
The sun does descend,
And our sports have an end:

Round the laps of their mothers,
Many sisters and brothers,
Like birds in their nest,
Are ready for rest;
And sport no more seen,
On the darkening Green.

'The Echoing Green' from the *Songs of Innocence* is a poem full of harmony, joy and happiness. It describes an idyllic setting in which humanity and nature, young and old, are in complete and utter harmony – a far cry, as we shall see, from 'The Garden of Love' from *Songs of Experience*. Just compare the two illustrations: in 'The Echoing Green', the people's arms and legs are open and expansive – they are moving; by contrast in 'The Garden of Love' the priest and the two children are cramped and kneeling at prayer – they are static.

Commentary

'The Garden of Love' is a simple poem in many ways: its vocabulary and syntax are straightforward. However, it masks profound ideas about religion and religious teaching, and their pernicious effects on human sexuality. It is also a poem that deals with the passage from innocence to experience as the speaker becomes aware of death.

The 'green' in the garden symbolizes the playing place of childhood (unencumbered by sex and religion) which in this poem comes under the rule of religion. Blake's illustrations are informative here: in 'The Echoing Green' we see an idyllic pastoral scene with children and some adults dancing and playing in harmony; by contrast, the illustration to 'The Garden of Love' is dominated by a priest leading two children in prayer – they are kneeling in a submissive pose.

'The Garden of Love' is an ironic title, because the poem is filled with negative imagery and 'love' is repressed. In the first stanza the speaker relates how he went to the Garden of Love and 'saw what I never had seen' – the wording here suggests that the Chapel has always been there but the speaker has only just noticed it.

The Chapel is hardly welcoming – the gates are shut and 'Thou shalt not' is written over the door. The Old Testament is relevant here: the Ten Commandments are also known as the Decalogue and, of the Decalogue, 7 out of 10 Commandments begin 'Thou shalt not' – an overwhelmingly negative set of commandments, telling you what you cannot do instead of what you can.

In despair and halfway through the second stanza the speaker turns to the Garden of Love itself 'That so many sweet flowers bore'.

But in the third and final stanza he discovers that

....*it was filled with graves,*

And tombstones where flowers should be.

The innocent green of childhood has been transformed into a place of death. And there is worse to come: the poem ends

And Priests in black gowns, were walking their rounds,

And binding with briars, my joys and desires.

The priests (always a loaded. pejorative word for Blake because of its associations with organized religion) wear the color of death and 'walking their rounds' suggests a deliberate act of surveillance – on the look out for anyone enjoying themselves or making love. The last two lines are longer than the other lines: perhaps this is to suggest the length of time it takes the priests to walk their rounds, spying on what is going on. The last two lines also include internal rhyme (gowns/rounds & briars/desires) which has the effect of the reader feeling trapped within the line – just as the speaker is.

For Blake, established, conventional religion had got it all wrong. He saw the God of the Old Testament (responsible for the Decalogue and all the repressive rules governing human behaviour) as the root of all evil. By contrast, Blake saw the God of the New Testament, Jesus, as the heart of Christianity, full of love, pity and compassion. Blake's poetry and religious views are somewhat esoteric, but if you want to learn more and if you've liked Blake – read more Blake.

In many ways, this poem is not typical of the love poems in the Anthology. Most of the poems are based on an intimate relationship between a man and a woman. The speaker in Blake's poem, however, addresses himself to a wider audience to show the egregious effect of the Church's moral laws and their pernicious effect on love – especially among the young. The poem has wider political and social concerns which make it stand out from the rest of the Anthology.

Why?

In this poem Blake

- charts the change from the sweet flowers of innocence to the tombstones of experience;
- presents natural love as being repressed by the laws and prohibitions of religion;
- writes an excoriating attack on priests and the church they represent.

Further reading:

The Songs of Innocence and of Experience ISBN: 978-1491281413

The Marriage of Heaven and Hell ISBN: 978-1495923869

Auguries of Innocence ISBN: 978-1495380877

The Illustrated Songs of Innocence (in colour) ISBN: 978-1492386629

The Illustrated Songs of Experience (in colour) ISBN: 978-1492707424

'Ae Fond Kiss' – Robert Burns

Ae fond kiss, and then we sever;
Ae fareweel, and then forever!
Deep in heart-wrung tears   I'll pledge thee,
Warring sighs and groans I'll wage thee.

Who shall say that Fortune grieves him,
While the star of hope she leaves him?
Me, nae cheerfu' twinkle lights me;
Dark despair around benights me.

I'll ne'er blame my partial fancy,
Naething could resist my Nancy;
But to see her was to love her;
Love but her, and love forever.

Had we never lov'd sae kindly,
Had we never lov'd sae blindly,
Never met—or never parted—
We had ne'er been broken-hearted.

Fare thee weel, thou first and fairest!
Fare thee weel, thou best and dearest!
Thine be ilka joy and treasure,
Peace. enjoyment, love, and pleasure!

Ae fond kiss, and then we sever;
Ae fareweel, alas, forever!
Deep in heart-wrung tears   I'll pledge thee,
Warring sighs and groans I'll wage thee!

Author & Context

Robert Burns (25 January 1759 – 21 July 1796) (also known as Robbie Burns, Rabbie Burns, Scotland's favourite son, the Ploughman Poet, Robden of Solway Firth, the Bard of Ayrshire and in Scotland as The Bard) was a Scottish poet and lyricist.

He is widely regarded as the national poet of Scotland and is celebrated worldwide. He is the best known of the poets who have written in the Scots language, although much of his writing is also in English and a light Scots dialect, accessible to an audience beyond Scotland. He also wrote in standard English, and in these writings his political or civil commentary is often at its bluntest. He is regarded as a pioneer of the Romantic movement, and after his death he became a great source of inspiration to the founders and creators of both liberalism and socialism, and a cultural icon in Scotland and among the Scottish Diaspora around the world. His own upbringing as the son of a tenant farmer and some years as a tenant farmer himself gave him a natural empathy with the poor and the marginalized in society, and this is reflected in the broadly egalitarian sentiments found in his poetry.

Ae – one

sever - part

pledge – toast

wage - give

benights – covers me in darkness and sadness

sae - so

ilka – every

Who? Burns speaks as himself to Mrs Agnes McLehose with whom he had a platonic, non-sexual relationship.

When? Burns sent her the poem on 27th of December 1791 just before she left Scotland to join her husband in Jamaica.

Where? Edinburgh.

What? Burns deeply laments their parting and wishes her every joy and happiness in the future, knowing that they will never meet again. The overall tone is one of deep melancholy.

Commentary

After the publication of his collected poems, the Kilmarnock volume, Burns regularly travelled and stayed ln Edinburgh. While there he established a platonic relationship with Mrs Agnes MacLehose and they began a regular correspondence using the pseudonyms 'Clarinda' and 'Sylvander'. Burns wrote 'Ae fond kiss' after their final meeting and sent it to Mrs McLehose on 27 December 1791 before she departed Edinburgh for Jamaica to be re-united with her husband.

In terms of the Anthology this poem is not typical in several ways. Firstly, it is based on a platonic, non-sexual relationship and deals with love as a deep and devoted friendship. Secondly, it is a song of farewell – given the state of transport in the late eighteenth century, Burns knows he will probably never see Mrs McLehose again. Thirdly, Burns chooses to write the poem in trochaic tetrameters and this falling rhythm is appropriate for the sad and mournful tone of the poem. Even here there is a paradox – the poem is full of sadness at the loss of such a close friend, but it also celebrates the close friendship that it simultaneously mourns. Finally, it is the only poem in the Anthology by a non-English writer, and Burns uses some variant spellings to suggest the Scottish accent as well as some words which had a specific meaning in Scots.

In the first stanza Burns asserts that they *sever* after one final *fond kiss* – and it is final – *forever*. He says he will toast her with *heart-wrung tears* and give her *warring sighs and groans*.

The second stanza says that Fortune cannot completely depress an individual while it leaves him with the star of hope, but for Burns there is no hope of meeting Mrs McLehose again:

Me nae cheerful twinkle lights me;

Dark despair around benights me.

His despair at parting from his friend is total and overwhelming.

In the third stanza Burns states that his despair is not his fault and that his love for his friend is not to be blamed for his mood of total despair. His feelings were not a *partial fancy*, because *Naething could resist my Nancy,* and in the second half of the stanza he claims

But to see her, was to love her,

Love but her, and love forever.

I cannot think of another poem in the Anthology which asserts so unequivocally one person's love for another – and we should remember that this is a poem about the love of friendship.

In the fourth stanza Burns admits that their current state of sadness and deep despair is only so deep because of the depth of their love for each other: if they had never met, they would not have to endure the pain of parting. However, if they had not met they would never have *lov'd sae kindly* and *blindly*.

Burns says farewell in the fifth and penultimate stanza, calling Mrs McLehore *first and fairest* and *best and dearest*. Then in a spirit of loving generosity he wishes her

.... *ilka joy and treasure,*

Peace, Enjoyment, Love and Pleasure.

The final verse repeats the first verse and this enchanting poem of deep and sincere friendship comes full circle.

Why?

In this poem Burns:

- expresses his despair and sadness at being parted forever from a dear friend;

- praises Mrs Mc Lehose and claims that anyone who knows her will fall in love with her;

- implies a deep and enduring friendship with the recipient of the poem;

- generously and graciously wishes her every joy and happiness in the future;

- uses the trochaic, falling rhythm to suggest sadness.

'She Walks in Beauty' – Lord Byron

She walks in beauty, like the night
    Of cloudless climes and starry skies;
And all that's best of dark and bright
    Meet in her aspect and her eyes;
Thus mellowed to that tender light
    Which heaven to gaudy day denies.

One shade the more, one ray the less,
    Had half impaired the nameless grace
Which waves in every raven tress,
    Or softly lightens o'er her face;
Where thoughts serenely sweet express,
    How pure, how dear their dwelling-place.

And on that cheek, and o'er that brow,
    So soft, so calm, yet eloquent,
The smiles that win, the tints that glow,
    But tell of days in goodness spent,
A mind at peace with all below,
    A heart whose love is innocent!

Author and Context

Lord George Gordon Byron (1788-1824) was as famous in his lifetime for his personality cult as for his poetry. He created the concept of the 'Byronic hero' - a defiant, melancholy young man, brooding on some mysterious, unforgivable event in his past. Byron's influence on European poetry, music, novel, opera, and painting has been immense, although the poet was widely condemned on moral grounds by his some of his contemporaries.

George Gordon, Lord Byron, was the son of Captain John Byron, and Catherine Gordon. He was born with a club-foot and became extreme sensitive about his lameness. Byron spent his early childhood years in poor surroundings in Aberdeen, where he was educated until he was ten. After he inherited the title and property of his great-uncle in 1798, he went on to Dulwich, Harrow, and Cambridge, where he piled up debts and aroused alarm with bisexual love affairs. Staying at Newstead in 1802, he probably first met his half-sister, Augusta Leigh with whom he was later suspected of having an incestuous relationship.

In 1807 Byron's first collection of poetry, *Hours of Idleness* appeared. It received bad reviews. The poet answered his critics with the satire *English Bards and Scotch Reviewers* in 1808. Next year he took his seat in the House of Lords, and set out on his grand tour, visiting Spain, Malta, Albania, Greece, and the Aegean. Real poetic success came in 1812 when Byron published the first two cantos of *Childe Harold's Pilgrimage* (1812-1818). He became an adored character of London society; he spoke in the House of Lords effectively on liberal themes, and had a hectic love-affair with Lady Caroline Lamb. Byron's *The Corsair* (1814), sold 10,000 copies on the first day of publication. He married Anne Isabella Milbanke in 1815, and their daughter Ada was born in the same year. The marriage was unhappy, and they obtained legal separation next year.

When the rumours started to rise of his incest and debts were accumulating, Byron left England in 1816, never to return. He settled in Geneva with Percy Bysshe Shelley, Mary Wollstonecraft Shelley, and Claire Clairmont, who became his mistress. There he wrote the two cantos of *Childe Harold* and "The Prisoner of Chillon". At the end of the summer Byron continued his travels, spending two years in Italy. During his years in Italy, Byron wrote *Lament of Tasso*, inspired by his visit to Tasso's cell in Rome, *Mazeppa* and started *Don Juan*, his satiric masterpiece.

After a long creative period, Byron had come to feel that action was more important than poetry. He armed a brig, the Hercules, and sailed to Greece to aid the Greeks, who had risen against their Ottoman overlords. However, before he saw any serious military action, Byron contracted a fever from which he died in Missolonghi on 19 April 1824. Memorial services were held all over the land. Byron's body was returned to England but was refused burial by the deans of both Westminster and St Paul's. Finally, Byron's coffin was placed in the family vault at Hucknall Torkard, near Newstead Abbey in Nottinghamshire.

climes – a country or region.

raven – a bird with jet black plumage.

tress – a plait or braid of hair.

o'er - over.

Who? Byron writes as himself. The poem is about Mrs John Wilmot, who was in mourning and was Byron's cousin by marriage.

When? Sometime in 1813 – it is said that Byron wrote the poem the morning after meeting Mrs Wilmot and it was published in *Hebrew Melodies* in 1814.

Where? At night at an evening function.

What? The poet praises the lady's beauty and links it to the purity of her character.

Commentary

"She Walks in Beauty" is a poem written in 1813 by Lord Byron, and is one of his most famous works. It was one of several poems to be set to Jewish tunes from the synagogue by Isaac Nathan, which were published as *Hebrew Melodies* in 1815.

It is said to have been inspired by an event in Byron's life: while at a ball, Byron met Anne Hathaway (Mrs Wilmot), his cousin by marriage through John Wilmot. She was in mourning, wearing a black dress set with spangles, as in the opening lines;

> *She walks in beauty, like the night*
> *Of cloudless climes and starry skies*

He was struck by her unusual beauty, and the next morning the poem was written.

'She Walks in Beauty' is not typical of the love poems in the Anthology, because it is largely descriptive. Indeed, it is a poem in which we get a sense of what the woman looks like and what she is wearing. Furthermore, most of the poems in the Anthology are very intimate: the poet addresses the female recipient of the poem. But not in this poem: the speaker's audience is anyone who reads the poem. Byron's poem attempts to praise the appearance and moral purity of the woman he is writing about – and as such is not typical of the other poems in the Anthology. In most of the other poems we learn little about the woman involved, but that is not true of Byron's poem. In many of the poems in the Anthology there is an emphasis on the poet's feelings: in Byron's poem his feelings are implied perhaps, but completely subservient to his description of the woman the poem is about. Unusually for the poems in the Anthology we get a real sense of what the woman is like. Byron's feelings towards her are not like several of the poems in the Anthology where the male writers are obsessed with their feelings or seducing the woman into bed. The poem comes across as objective praise by a disinterested observer. Furthermore, it also subverts the convention that beautiful women have fair hair and are blonde in complexion – although many of Shakespeare's sonnets are addressed to the so-called Dark Lady of the sonnets.

The poem is written in iambic tetrameters with only one variation the opening trochaic foot of line 4.

Byron begins the poem with a simple simile: Mrs Wilmot is like the night and the alliteration in the second line foregrounds the image still further. Byron then indulges in hyperbole by claiming that

All that's best of dark and bright

Meet in her aspect and her eyes.

She is lit by moonlight and starlight which Byron which Byron calls a *tender light* which is denied to *gaudy day*, gaudy being used pejoratively.

The second stanza stresses the absolute perfection of her appearance:

One shade the more, one ray the less

would have *impaired* the beauty of this woman. Byron claims she has a *nameless grace/Which waves in every raven tress* and he links her external beauty with her inner thoughts and feelings, claiming that in her face one can discern

... thoughts serenely sweet [which] express

How pure, how dear their dwelling place.

The third stanza is full of praise for the recipient of the poem. Byron says that on her *cheeks* and on her *brow* - which are *so soft, so calm, yet eloquent,* are

The smiles that win, the tints that glow,

But tell of days in goodness spent.

In short, according to Byron's poem, she is the perfect woman: perfect in looks and in personality, character and intellect. She has

A mind at peace with all below,

A heart whose love is innocent.

Why is this such a famous poem?

- Byron acts as an objective observer so we are more likely to believe him;
- the regular iambic tetrameters do not distract from the harmony of the woman he describes – in fact, they enhance it and make it easy to memorize;
- the night-time setting is romantic and links with Mrs Wilmot's hair and complexion;
- the language is simple and easy to understand;
- Byron uses alliteration throughout but in an unobtrusive way;

- Byron establishes a clear link between the woman's beauty and her character – something unique in this Anthology.

Further reading: *Hebrew Melodies* ISBN: 978-1511897449

'Remember' – Christina Rossetti

Remember me when I am gone away,
    Gone far away into the silent land;
    When you can no more hold me by the hand,
Nor I half turn to go yet turning stay.
Remember me when no more day by day
    You tell me of our future that you plann'd:
    Only remember me; you understand
It will be late to counsel then or pray.
Yet if you should forget me for a while
    And afterwards remember, do not grieve:
    For if the darkness and corruption leave
    A vestige of the thoughts that once I had,
Better by far you should forget and smile
    Than that you should remember and be sad.

Author & Context

Christina Rossetti was born in 1830 into a highly talented family – all of whom wrote or painted – and Rossetti was encouraged by her family to pursue her artistic talents from an early age. Her father, a poet and translator, lived in exile, and the family were held together by the mother who had a very strong Christian faith. Rossetti's poetry revolves around the themes of love and death, and there is often a strong religious dimension to her work. Her own life was increasingly unhappy: she was engaged to be married twice, but broke off both engagements. She suffered terrible ill-health, although she continued to write, and her final years were darkened by the deaths of most of her family and her two previous lovers. She died in 1894, having achieved much acclaim for her writing. She never married despite being engaged three times – the weddings were all called off.

vestige – tiny remnant, trace.

Who? The speaker of the poem speaks directly to a friend or friends and tells them how to behave in the event of her death.

When? No particular setting.

Where? No specific location.

What? Rossetti gives her friend advice on how to remember her when she is dead.

Commentary

This type of poem, instructing a loved one how to react to death, is unique in the Anthology but not in English Literature. Compare, for example, Shakespeare's Sonnet 71:

SONNET 71

No longer mourn for me when I am dead
Then you shall hear the surly sullen bell
Give warning to the world that I am fled
From this vile world, with vilest worms to dwell:
Nay, if you read this line, remember not
The hand that writ it; for I love you so
That I in your sweet thoughts would be forgot
If thinking on me then should make you woe.
O, if, I say, you look upon this verse
When I perhaps compounded am with clay,
Do not so much as my poor name rehearse.
But let your love even with my life decay,
   Lest the wise world should look into your moan

And mock you with me after I am gone.

By contrast Rossetti's poem is more intimate and gains its power through the use of imperatives: *Remember* and *forget*. On the surface the poem is all about death, but the very act of setting free of the addressee of the poem implies a strong love and compassion and empathy for the person the poem is addressed to.

The poem is a Petrarchan sonnet: the first quatrain is one sentence long as is the second quatrain; there is a conventional turn of volta in line 9 which changes the direction of the thought and the sestet is one sentence long. With occasional variation the poem is written in iambic pentameters. *Only* in line 7 and *Better* in line 13 are trochaic feet which draw our attention to these important words.

Rossetti was only 19 when she wrote this poem, and it may have been influenced by her father who suffered very bad health.

The poem is characterized by its brave and stoical tone, and the love that is implied to the addressee. The poem starts with a simple instruction, delivered as an imperative:

Remember me when I am gone away.

The speaker's attitude towards death remains calm and collected and she sees death with equanimity:

Gone far away into the silent land;

When you can no more hold me by the hand,

Nor I half turn to go yet turning stay.

These lines suggest an intimacy between the speaker and the person to whom the poem is addressed: are they lovers? The intimacy of tone would suggest so, as would the holding of hands.

In the second quatrain Rossetti keeps her calm control over the tone:

Remember me when no more day by day

You tell me of our future that you planned.

The fact that they have a future and are making plans for it suggests a straightforward love affair, but the recipient of the poem is in charge – he makes the plans, while Rossetti remains a passive recipient of them. However, the plans suggest a future together that he has planned. This is not a casual affair but serious love. However, we see in the fact that HE has planned their future the lack of power that women suffered in the Victorian period. Perhaps that explains *why she half turn[s] to go yet turning* stay – as if she is unhappy to cede all control over their future plans to him.

Line 7 begins with another imperative – *Only remember me* - and this is followed by a strong caesura which emphasizes the finality of death: once she is dead *It will be late to counsel then or pray.*

In line 9 comes the volta or turn, and Rossetti signals the change of tone and subject matter with *Yet*. Rossetti states in a perfect example of love and compassion towards the recipient of the poem:

...if you should forget me for a while

And afterwards remember. Do not grieve.

As Sonnet 71 by Shakespeare, Rossetti urges her lover not to worry if he forgets to grieve, because, as the final two lines express it:

Better by far you should forget and smile

Than that you should remember and be sad.

Rossetti relinquishes her lover from any obligation to think of her. She does not want her memory to cause him any more pain. He should not feel guilty for forgetting her if remembering her causes him distress and anguish, although the word remember is used four times in the sonnet.

Parts of the sestet are gloomy and pessimistic in the face of death: Rossetti paints a vivid picture of what we are to expect after death – *the darkness and corruption* – which may only leave

A vestige of the thoughts that I once had.

That is the most we can hope for in death: a vestige.

Overall the sonnet is slow and stately in its rhythm with the exception on lines 11 and 12, where Rossetti seems to be running towards death.

This poem is not very typical of the other poems in the Anthology. It is the only poem written by a woman in the pre-1900 Anthology. It has no erotic moments and concentrates on death not love. The lack of eroticism is probably due to Victorian morality and the power it exerted over Victorian literary mores. However, that does not mean the poem lacks intimacy, rather that its intimacy is subdued.

Why?

In this poem Rossetti

- gives clear instructions to her lover in the event of her death;
- displays great generosity of spirit in the sestet of the sonnet which implies great love for the recipient of the poem;
- is atypical of the poems in the Anthology in its reticence about sex and romantic love – it could even be addressed to a close friend.

Further reading: *Essential Poems* 978-1511935869

'The Ruined Maid' – Thomas Hardy

"O 'Melia, my dear, this does everything crown!
Who could have supposed I should meet you in Town?
And whence such fair garments, such prosperi-ty?" —
"O didn't you know I'd been ruined?" said she.

— "You left us in tatters, without shoes or socks,
Tired of digging potatoes, and spudding up docks;
And now you've gay bracelets and bright feathers three!" —
"Yes: that's how we dress when we're ruined," said she.

— "At home in the barton you said thee' and thou,'
And 'thik oon' and 'theäs oon' and 't'other'; but now
Your talking quite fits 'ee for high compa-ny!" —
"Some polish is gained with one's ruin," said she.

— "Your hands were like paws then, your face blue and bleak
But now I'm bewitched by your delicate cheek,
And your little gloves fit as on any la-dy!" —
"We never do work when we're ruined," said she.

— "You used to call home-life a hag-ridden dream,
And you'd sigh, and you'd sock; but at present you seem
To know not of megrims or melancho-ly!" —
"True. One's pretty lively when ruined," said she.

— "I wish I had feathers, a fine sweeping gown,
And a delicate face, and could strut about Town!" —
"My dear — a raw country girl, such as you be,
Cannot quite expect that. You ain't ruined," said she.

Context

Thomas Hardy (1840 – 1928) is best known as a novelist. He wrote 15 novels, most of which are set largely in Dorset and the surrounding counties, and which deal with the ordinary lives of ordinary people in stories in which they struggle to find happiness and love – often battling against fate or their own circumstances. His final two novels *Tess of the D'Urbervilles* (1891) and *Jude the Obscure* (1895) both portray sex outside marriage in a sympathetic way and there was such a hysterical public outcry about the novels that Hardy stopped writing fiction and devoted the rest of his life to poetry. Although some of his poetry is intensely personal, this poem is also typical of his work in that it gives a voice to two ordinary women. Despite the horrified reaction to his last two novels, there was a thriving sex industry in Victorian Britain, and, for many working class girls, prostitution was their only means of survival.

Melia – a shortened form of Amelia, but cleverly chosen by Hardy: Melia is an ironic pun on the Latin word *melior* which means better. It is ironic because, although Melia's material conditions have improved, her moral and social status have been destroyed by her occupation.

this does everything crown – this is better than anything else.

garments – clothes.

tatters – rags.

spudding up docks – digging up crops.

barton – farmyard.

thee, thou – you.

thik oon – that one.

theas oon – this one.

t'other – the other.

Ee – he.

hag-ridden – plagued by evil spirits.

sock – to suck, to take a short and sharp intake of breath – the opposite of a sigh.

megrims – migraines.

melancholy – sadness, depression.

Who? Two young women, who were once acquaintances, talk to each other. In the past they have worked as agricultural labourers, but 'Melia has moved to a town and now lives a life of ease, working as a prostitute or perhaps as a mistress to one man.

When? Late Victorian Britain.

Where? In 'town' – 'Melia has moved to town while her acquaintance has continued to live and work in the countryside.

What? The poem consists of a dialogue between the two girls.

Commentary

This poem consists of six quatrains all of which (except the last) are organized in the same way. The first girl – whose name we never know and who lives and works in the countryside – addresses her friend in the first three lines of the quatrain; in the final line of each stanza, 'Melia, who used to work with her friend but who now lives in Town, answers. In her responses 'Melia always uses the word *ruin* or some version of it. *Town* seems to be the nearest large city in the farming area that the young women live in; it might even be London.

The opening stanza establishes that 'Melia has undergone a change of routine since they last met: her friend comments on her fair garments and her apparent prosperity. Note how Hardy prints *prosperi-ty*: he is gently mocking the friend's pronunciation of the word, so that we are forced to put the stress of the word, unnaturally, on the final syllable, and, of course, by stressing the final syllable he is emphasizing its rhyme with the fourth line. This mispronunciation also occurs in lines 11, 15 and 19.

The second stanza gives us more detail about the life 'Melia used to live in the countryside. Her clothes were poor and she worked on the land, doing heavy manual labour. Now, however, her dress has improved: she has *gay bracelets* and wears three fine feathers in her hat.

In the third stanza the speaker draws attention to the way 'Melia's speech has changed. When she worked in the fields she used antiquated dialect forms of speech, but now her speech has changed and has given her some *polish*. She has changed her way of talking now she has left her old life behind.

The details in the fourth stanza give us a hint of the reality of hard manual labour on a farm. 'Melia's hands used to be *like paws* and her face was *blue and bleak* from working outside, exposed to all the weather of every season. Living in town has softened her skin and her hands are like a lady's – not hardened and roughened by work.

'Melia's mood has changed too: she is no longer plagued by depression, sadness and migraines. 'Melia admits in the final line that now she is *pretty lively*.

The final stanza changes the pattern of the previous five. In this stanza the unnamed friend from the country speaks only the first two lines (instead of the first three) and 'Melia has a two line response. The friend wishes that she could live the same life as 'Melia, enjoy the same material comforts and strut about Town. But 'Melia points out that her friend cannot - because she is not ruined. Note the use of the word *ain't* in the final line: this shows that 'Melia has not really acquired all the polish that her friend thinks she has. The word reveals that despite the superficial changes she has undergone, she still uses speech which considered wrong and ungrammatical.

You should note that Hardy is a master of poetic techniques. Many lines are given added power by alliteration, assonance and consonance or the use of simple similes – *like paws*.

At the heart of this poem is the word *ruin*. This is actually a poem about prostitution in Victorian England. In public the Victorians were very straight-laced and uptight about sex, but in reality it has been estimated that 20% of the adult female population were prostitutes or someone's mistress. It is unclear whether 'Melia is a prostitute with numerous clients or whether she is mistress to one wealthy, married man, but what is clear is that all the changes in her life have come from selling her body. The bracelets and the three feathers are the signs of her trade.

To be *ruined* in Victorian Britain meant to have lost your virginity before marriage. 'Melia is ruined in the sense that she will no longer be able to get married in a respectable way because of her occupation. The irony is that, despite the implications of the word, meaning to be spoilt forever, she is actually living a much better life than she did as a farm labourer. Hardy is exposing Victorian hypocrisy about sex in this poem. He is also attacking the class system of his day. 'Melia has no other way to become better off and live a materially better life than to sell her body. Victorian society kept women, especially working class women, in subservient positions. Women like 'Melia have no access to education or the professions and therefore the only alternative to being a farm labourer is to become a prostitute. Through her acquaintance's words we get a vivid picture of how hard life as a farm labourer must have been and so it is natural that 'Melia's friend (who does not appear to understand exactly what 'Melia does in order to dress so well) envies 'Melia her new-found wealth – her improved speech, clothes, mood and complexion. So women had a limited choice: they could become morally ruined as 'Melia has done or they can remain financially and physically ruined by remaining as a farm worker.

'Melia's own attitude to her change of circumstances is hard to read. She seems proud of her new clothes and new ways of talking; she says that she lives a *lively* life and boasts that she does not have to work. However, you may detect in her final speech a sense of regret that in order to have a better standard of living she has had to sell her body.

Hardy's own attitude is also hard to discern, especially as he has no voice within the poem: he presents the dialogue without authorial comment. However, if you were to read his later novels I think you would be able to work out that Hardy sympathizes with both women. He is very sympathetic to Tess in *Tess of the D'Urbervilles* who loses her virginity through rape and then, when she is later married to another man, is condemned by him for not being a virgin! Hardy seems sympathetic to the acquaintance because of the back-breaking work she has to do as a farm worker, and he extends his sympathy to 'Melia too - who is condemned by society and seen as *ruined* when that is her only option to get a better life. This is hypocrisy because Victorian society condemns working class women to manual labour and also condemns 'Melia and women like her who become prostitutes – but prostitutes who are used by 'respectable' wealthy men. If society were fairer, Hardy seems to be saying, then women would have the chance to escape from manual labour without having to sell their bodies. It is interesting that the title does not make clear which of the two women is ruined – in a sense, they both are.

However, on the surface this is a casual, almost light-hearted poem which in a way reflects the fact that this is a conversation between two acquaintances – one of whom does not understand the true nature of the situation and the other who does not want to reveal fully the truth of what she does. As I have said above, it all hinges on the word *ruined*.

You may think it is unusual for a poem about prostitution or being a kept woman, a wealthy man's mistress to be in an Anthology of love poems, but bought love is still a type of love. Certainly it is not typical of the poems in the Anthology – not least because the two speaking voices are female not male. This gives Hardy the opportunity to present the views of women and to draw attention to male exploitation of woman in Victorian society. As such it is a searing attack on Victorian patriarchal and hypocritical attitudes summed up in the word *ruined*, and the way love is debased by money in Victorian society.

Why?

In this superficially straightforward poem written in largely everyday language, Hardy

- expresses sympathy for the plight of Victorian working class women;

- attacks Victorian attitudes to class and sex;

- reveals the hypocrisy at the heart of respectable society;

- uses the ordinary, everyday language of working class women and so gives a voice to an oppressed social group ignored by mainstream literature;

- shows the sordid reality of 'love' for poor, working class women.

Further reading: *Poems of the Past and the Present* ISBN: 978-1495918653

'At an Inn' – Thomas Hardy

When we as strangers sought
Their catering care,
Veiled smiles bespoke their thought
Of what we were.
They warmed as they opined
Us more than friends--
That we had all resigned
For love's dear ends.

And that swift sympathy
With living love
Which quicks the world--maybe
The spheres above,
Made them our ministers,
Moved them to say,
"Ah, God, that bliss like theirs
Would flush our day!"

And we were left alone
As Love's own pair;
Yet never the love-light shone
Between us there!
But that which chilled the breath
Of afternoon,
And palsied unto death
The pane-fly's tune.

The kiss their zeal foretold,
And now deemed come,
Came not: within his hold

Love lingered numb.
Why cast he on our port
A bloom not ours?
Why shaped us for his sport
In after-hours?

As we seemed we were not
That day afar,
And now we seem not what
We aching are.
O severing sea and land,
O laws of men,
Ere death, once let us stand
As we stood then!

Author & Context

Thomas Hardy (1840 – 1928) is best known as a novelist. He wrote 15 novels, most of which are set largely in Dorset and the surrounding counties, and which deal with the ordinary lives of ordinary people in stories in which they struggle to find happiness and love – often battling against fate or their own circumstances. His final two novels *Tess of the D'Urbervilles* (1891) and *Jude the Obscure* (1895) both portray sex outside marriage in a sympathetic way and there was such a hysterical public outcry about the novels that Hardy stopped writing fiction and devoted the rest of his life to poetry.

bespoke – made clear, made evident.

opined – to form or express an opinion.

quicks – gives life to.

the spheres above – before we understood the nature of the universe through the work of Galileo and Newton, it was believed that the Earth was at the centre of the universe and that it was surrounded by glass spheres in which were set the moon, the other planets and the stars. Hardy does not believe this at all, but is using poetic licence to suggest that Love is so powerful that it can help the spheres to move.

palsied – paralyzed.

pane-fly – a large fly rather like a bluebottle.

Who? The poet and a woman are out for the day and come across an inn where they have lunch, submitting to the *catering care* of the staff at the inn.

When? No time is specified but the action takes place in the past.

Where? At a country inn.

What? The staff at the inn assume that the poet and the woman are lovers, and, indeed, there was the possibility of that relationship developing – but (much to Hardy's regret) their relationship did not flourish.

Commentary

This is an extraordinarily delicate and sensitive poem about a love affair that did not quite happen. Until the unalloyed passion of the final stanza, it is a highly nuanced poem – appropriate for its subject of a love and passion that did not materialize. Hardy writes in a strict pattern, each stanza has the same rhyme scheme: the odd lines are trimeters (three stresses) and the even lines are dimeters (two stresses). The strictness of this scheme would suggest Hardy's control over his feelings about the incident – which are full of regret as the final stanza shows. The short even lines are appropriate as they suggest something unfinished, something incomplete – and by the fourth stanza we know that their love (the conditions for which seemed so propitious) came to nothing. Hardy uses the same rhyme scheme in each stanza – more evidence of his control over his emotions.

In the first stanza Hardy and his female companion arrive at an inn and they have a meal – submitting themselves to the *catering care* of the staff at the inn. The staff assume that Hardy and his companion are lovers and their *veiled smiles* reflect their vicarious happiness at serving a couple in love.

They warmed as they opined
Us more than friends –
That we had all resigned
For loves dear ends.

In the second stanza the staff display *swift sympathy* with what they see as *living love* – and Hardy foregrounds the central importance of love in human affairs when he writes that love *quicks the world – maybe/The spheres above*. The assumption that Hardy and his companion are lovers makes the staff their ministers and makes them reflect

"Ah, God, that bliss like theirs
Would flush our day!"

The third stanza, however, marks a change in tone. The staff of the inn still see them as *Love's own pair*, but things do not go to plan for reasons Hardy does not give:

Yet never the love-light shone

Between us there!

What passed between Hardy and his companion *chilled the breath/Of afternoon/And palsied unto death/The pane-fly's tune.*

The *zeal* and enthusiasm of the staff of the inn had foretold a kiss, but a kiss did not materialize and *Love lingered numb.* Hardy then personifies love to ask why love and a greater intimacy did not develop:

Why cast he on our port
A bloom not ours?
Why shaped us for his sport
In after hours?

There is a time-shift to the present in the fifth stanza: Hardy speaks of the excursion to the inn as *that day afar.* He starts by stating that they *seemed [as] we were not,* and as the staff at the inn had assumed they were. However, he is upset by the memory and the fact that they did not fall in love:

...now we seem not what
We aching are.

That word 'aching' suggests a deep sadness about the failure of the relationship. Now they are separated by distance (*severing sea and land*) or by being married to other people (*the laws of men*). The final two lines of the poem express the wish that before they die they can go back to the atmosphere and level of feelings they had when they first arrived at the inn:

Ere death, once let us stand

As we stood then!

The exclamation indicates how upset Hardy is and how much he desires their reunion – despite its unlikelihood given what separates them now.

Why?

In this poem Hardy

- writes sensitively about a relationship that did not develop into love;
- the assumption made by the staff of the inn (that Hardy and his companion are in love) makes the reality of the situation even more ironic;
- writes a poignant story of love unfulfilled;
- reveals the anguish and despair that their relationship did not develop into love;
- is restrained in the first four stanzas but lets his real feelings pour out in the final stanza, looking back on the incident many years later.

Further reading: *Wessex Poems and Other Verses* ISBN: 978-1495463013

'La Belle Dame sans Merci: A Ballad' – John Keats

I

O what can ail thee, knight-at-arms,
  Alone and palely loitering?
The sedge has wither'd from the lake,
  And no birds sing.

II

O what can ail thee, knight-at-arms!
  So haggard and so woe-begone?
The squirrel's granary is full,
  And the harvest's done.

III

I see a lily on thy brow
  With anguish moist and fever dew,
And on thy cheeks a fading rose
  Fast withereth too.

IV

I met a lady in the meads,
  Full beautiful—a faery's child,
Her hair was long, her foot was light,
  And her eyes were wild.

V

I made a garland for her head,
  And bracelets too, and fragrant zone;
She look'd at me as she did love,
  And made sweet moan.

VI

I set her on my pacing steed,
  And nothing else saw all day long,
For sidelong would she bend, and sing
  A faery's song.

VII

She found me roots of relish sweet,
  And honey wild, and manna dew,
And sure in language strange she said—
  "I love thee true."

VIII

She took me to her elfin grot,
  And there she wept, and sigh'd fill sore,
And there I shut her wild wild eyes
  With kisses four.

IX

And there she lulled me asleep,
  And there I dream'd—Ah! woe betide!

The latest dream I ever dream'd
On the cold hill's side.

X

I saw pale kings and princes too,
　Pale warriors, death-pale were they all;
They cried—"La Belle Dame sans Merci
　Hath thee in thrall!"

XI

I saw their starved lips in the gloam,
　With horrid warning gapèd wide,
And I awoke and found me here,
　On the cold hill's side.

XII

And this is why I sojourn here,
　Alone and palely loitering,
Though the sedge is withered from the lake,
　And no birds sing.

Author & Context

John Keats (31 October 1795 – 23 February 1821) was
an English Romantic poet. He was one of the main figures of the
second generation of Romantic poets along with Lord
Byron and Percy Bysshe Shelley, despite his work having been in

publication for only four years before his death. Although his poems were not generally well received by critics during his life, his reputation grew after his death, so that by the end of the 19th century, he had become one of the most beloved of all English poets. He had a significant influence on a diverse range of poets and writers.

The poetry of Keats is characterised by sensual imagery, most notably in the series of odes. Today his poems and letters are some of the most popular and most analysed in English literature. Keats suffered from tuberculosis, for which, at the time, there was no cure and as a result, perhaps, many of his poems are tinged with sadness and thoughts of mortality, as well as having a keen eye for the beauties of nature and the pains of unrequited love.

La Belle Dame sans Merci – the beautiful woman without pity.

what can ail thee – what can trouble or afflict you.

loitering -waiting around with no fixed purpose.

sedge – a type of grass whish flourishes in watery places.

woe-begone – consumed with woe and sadness.

meads – meadows and fields.

steed – his horse.

manna – delicious food for body and mind.

grot – a cave.

in thrall – to be held like a slave.

gloam – twilight, dusk.

sojourn – to stay for a period of time.

Who? An unidentified speaker asks a knight-at-arms what is wrong with him: he or she speaks for the first three stanzas. The knight then tells his story.

When? The knight and the people he sees in his dream suggest a medieval setting, centuries before Keats was alive.

Where? An indeterminate outdoor setting: the knight says he is on the cold hill's side and the setting is rural.

What? The knight met La Belle Dame Sans Merci of the title. They seemed to fall in love and she took him to her grot. He fell asleep and dreamt a dream before walking up on the cold hillside, alone and deeply sad.

Commentary

This is one of hundreds of anonymous ballads which were passed down orally before being written down.

Lady Maisrey

She called to her little pageboy,
Who was her brother's son.
She told him quick as he could go,
To bring her lord safe home.

Now the very first mile he would walk
And the second he would run,

And when he came to a broken, broken bridge,
He bent his breast and swum.

And when he came to the new castell,
The lord was set at meat;
If you were to know as much as I,
How little you would eat!

O is my tower falling, falling down,
Or does my bower burn?
Or is my gay lady put to bed
With a daughter or a son?

O no, your tower is not falling down,
Nor does your bower burn;
But we are afraid ere you return,
Your lady will be dead and gone.

Come saddle, saddle my milk-white steed,
Come saddle my pony too,
That I may neither eat nor drink,
Till I come to the old castell.

Now when he came to the old castell,
He heard a big bell toll;
And then he saw eight noble, noble men,
A bearing of a pall.

Lay down, lay down, that gentle, gentle corpse,
As it lay fast asleep,
That I may kiss her red ruby lips,
Which I used to kiss so sweet.

Six times he kissed her red ruby lips,
Nine times he kissed her chin.
Ten times he kissed her snowy, snowy breast,
Where love did enter in.

The lady was buried on that Sunday,
Before the prayer was done;
And the lord he died on the next Sunday,
Before the prayer begun.

I have included this anonymous ballad to give you a sense of the tradition Keats was drawing on when he wrote 'La Belle Dane Sans Merci'. It is also written in the traditional ballad stanza. I chose it also because it involves love and death, and a way of telling the story which is elliptical – in which important parts are left out and the readers are left to their own conclusions. Keats' poem is filled with such features.

"La Belle Dame sans Merci" is a popular form given an artistic sheen by the Romantic poets. Keats uses a stanza of three iambic tetrameter lines with the fourth line shortened which makes the stanza seem a self-contained unit, giving the ballad a deliberate and slow movement, and is pleasing to the ear although the short last line could also be argued to add an air of doubt, of uncertainty and incompleteness. Keats uses a number of the stylistic characteristics of the ballad, such as simplicity of language, repetition, and absence of details; like some of the old ballads, it deals with the supernatural. Keats's economical manner of telling a story in "La Belle Dame sans Merci" is the direct opposite of his lavish manner in "The Eve of St. Agnes". Part of the fascination exerted by the poem comes from Keats' use of understatement. It is a love story. The shortened last line suggests a lack of completeness and, as such, is appropriate to the events of the poem and the overall sense of melancholy and anguish that pervades it. The poem became famous in the Victorian period and several Pre-Raphaelite artists produced work inspired by the poem and reproduces here.

Keats sets his simple story of love and death in a bleak wintry landscape that is appropriate to it: *The sedge has wither'd from the lake/ And no birds sing!* The repetition of these two lines, with minor variations, as the concluding lines of the poem emphasizes the fate of the unfortunate knight and neatly encloses the poem in a frame by bringing it back to its beginning. Keats relates the condition of the trees and surroundings with the condition of the knight who is also broken.

In keeping with the ballad tradition, Keats does not identify his questioner, or the knight, or the destructively beautiful lady. What Keats does not include in his poem contributes as much to it in arousing the reader's imagination as what he puts into it. La belle dame sans merci, the beautiful lady without pity, is a femme fatale, a Circe-like figure who attracts lovers only to destroy them by her supernatural powers. She destroys because it is her nature to destroy. Keats could have found patterns for his "faery's child" in folk mythology, classical literature, Renaissance poetry, or the medieval ballad. With a few skilful touches, he creates a woman who is at once beautiful, erotically attractive, fascinating, and deadly.

Some readers see the poem as Keats' personal rebellion against the pains of love. In his letters and in some of his poems, he reveals that he did experience the pains, as well as the pleasures, of love and that he resented the pains, particularly the loss of freedom that came with falling in love. However, the ballad is a very objective form, and it may be best to read "La Belle Dame sans Merci" as pure story and no more. Certainly the poem stands out from the others in the Anthology by having a clear narrative element – although the sadness that love can cause is touched upon in several different poems.

The first three stanzas of the poem are spoken by an unidentified speaker who questions the knight-at-arms. It is winter and the knight is clearly unwell:

I

O what can ail thee, knight-at-arms,
  Alone and palely loitering?
The sedge has wither'd from the lake,
  And no birds sing.

II

O what can ail thee, knight-at-arms!
  So haggard and so woe-begone?

The squirrel's granary is full,
And the harvest's done.

III

I see a lily on thy brow
  With anguish moist and fever dew,
And on thy cheeks a fading rose
  Fast withereth too.

The lily is a flower associated with death, while on the knight's cheeks there is a *fading rose,* suggesting a fading or lost love. The questions serve the simple task of arousing the reader's interest, while the state of the knight is pitiful: he is *alone and palely loitering, haggard* and *woe-begone* and *anguish* is apparent on his fevered brow.

The knight then tells his story and how he has come to be in this situation. The knight met a lady *in the meads*; she was *full beautiful, a faery's child* (which introduces a supernatural element). It is clear that the knight is attracted to the woman and captivated by her appearance:

Her hair was long, her foot was light,

And her eyes were wild.

The knight shows his love for the woman by making a *garland* for her head and *bracelets* and

She looked at me as she did love,

And made sweet moan.

The word *as* is important in the quotation used above because it means she looked at him as if she did love him. In the next stanza the knight seems to take full possession of the woman by placing her on his *prancing steed* and his obsession and infatuation with the woman is total:

And nothing else saw all day long,

For sidelong would she bend, and sing

A faery's song.

The faery's child, the woman, feeds the knight on *roots of relish sweet,/And honey wild. And manna-dew*

and then

...in language strange she said –

'I love thee true'.

The next stanza represents the climax of their love:

She took me to her Elfin grot,

And there she wept and sighed full sore.

And there I shut her wild wild eyes

With kisses four.

The kisses four feel like a consummation of their love and they certainly calm the wildness in her eyes. The woman lulls him to sleep and then the knight has a disturbing dream: *Ah! Woe betide!:*

I saw pale kings and princes too'

Pale warriors, death-pale were they all

They cried – 'La belle dame sans merci

Hath thee in thrall!'

I saw their starved lips in the gloam,

With horrid warning gapèd wide,

And I awoke to find me here

On the hill's cold side.

Of course, the wintry, lifeless landscape, underlined by the repetition of the *hill's cold side* acts as a pathetic fallacy for the knight's sense of futility and despondency.

The final stanza reminds us of the barrenness of the landscape:

And this is why I sojourn here,
Alone and palely loitering,
Though the sedge is withered from the lake,
And no birds sing.

A key word in the final stanza is *this* in the first line. Is the knight hoping to meet La belle dame sans merci again, once more to come under her spell? Is he so broken by his experiences that he can do

nothing but palely loiter, enervated by the glimpse of love that he has seen but from which he is banished? Has his taste of love with the faery's child soured his feelings about love forever? Or has his taste of love left him bereft and lifeless until he tastes it again?

In his other poems Keats writes extensively about love. However, in 'La Belle Dame Merci', by choosing the impersonal ballad form, Keats distances himself personally from the poem and its sentiments. Nonetheless, a clear picture of love emerges through the unusual story of the knight and his encounter with La belle dame sans merci.

This poem is typical of some poems in the Anthology because it deals with the anguish and torment of unrequited love, but it is not typical in many more ways. It is set in a vague medieval past and the ballad form de-personalizes it and distances it from the poet's own feelings – most of the poems in the Anthology are deeply personal.

Why?

In this poem:

- Keats presents the anguish and torment of lost love;
- at the same time in in stanzas VI, VII and VIII Keats presents the alluring pleasures of romantic love;

- uses the ballad form to present an intriguing story of a haggard knight at arms who has been broken in some way by love;
- successfully imitates the traditional ballad through his use of the ballad stanza, repetition, hints of the supernatural, illogical turns of events and the anonymity of the speakers.

'Non sum qualis eram bonae sub regno Cynarae' – Ernest Dowson

Last night, ah, yesternight, betwixt her lips and mine
There fell thy shadow, Cynara! thy breath was shed
Upon my soul between the kisses and the wine;
And I was desolate and sick of an old passion,
    Yea, I was desolate and bowed my head:
I have been faithful to thee, Cynara! in my fashion.

All night upon mine heart I felt her warm heart beat,
Night-long within mine arms in love and sleep she lay;
Surely the kisses of her bought red mouth were sweet;
But I was desolate and sick of an old passion,
    When I awoke and found the dawn was grey:
I have been faithful to thee, Cynara! in my fashion.

I have forgot much, Cynara! gone with the wind,
Flung roses, roses riotously with the throng,
Dancing, to put thy pale, lost lilies out of mind,
But I was desolate and sick of an old passion,
    Yea, all the time, because the dance was long:
I have been faithful to thee, Cynara! in my fashion.

I cried for madder music and for stronger wine,
But when the feast is finished and the lamps expire,
Then falls thy shadow, Cynara! the night is thine;
And I am desolate and sick of an old passion,
    Yea, hungry for the lips of my desire:
I have been faithful to thee, Cynara! in my fashion.

Author & Context

Ernest Christopher Dowson (2 August 1867 – 23 February 1900) was an English poet, novelist, and short-story writer, often associated with the Decadent movement, which flourished in the 1880s and 1890s, reflecting a fin-de-siècle weariness with the strict rigidities of the prevailing Victorian conventions and mores. Born into a wealthy middle class family, he had a tragic life. His father died in 1894, followed the next year by the death of his mother by suicide. Dowson quickly descended into an alcohol-fuelled world of decadence and misery – which is reflected in his poems by a sense of regret, loss and grief for the past.

Non sum qualis eram bonae sub regno Cynarae – 'I am not as I was in the reign of good Cinara'. The title comes from the Roman poet Horace. In Horace he implores the goddess Venus not to allow himself to fall in love again – he is too old, he says, and love should be left to younger, more energetic men. Dowson's poem is completely different, but it is possible to trace some of Horace's world-weary sadness underlying Dowson's poem.

Dowson's work is typical of nineteenth century fin de siècle writing. Fin de siècle is French for end of the century, a term which typically encompasses both the meaning of the similar English idiom turn of the century and also makes reference to the closing of one era and onset of a new era. The term is typically used to refer to the end of the 19th century. This period was widely thought to be a period of degeneration, but at the same time a period of hope for a new beginning. The "spirit" of fin de siècle often refers to the cultural hallmarks that were recognized as prominent in the 1880s and 1890s, including ennui, cynicism, pessimism, and "...a widespread belief that civilization leads to decadence." The decadence of much fin de siècle writing is also due to a backlash against the restrictive morality of the Victorian period, a relaxation of public morals (certainly among writers and artists) and a belief in art for art's sake – as opposed to art for the sake of public education with all the didacticism that involves.

expire – go out.

Who? The speaker of the poem addresses a former lover – Cynara.

When? No specific time is mentioned, but the speaker, at certain points, appears to be waking up after a night in bed – which suggests a general setting of dawn.

Where? No particular location. In bed perhaps after a night of love.

What? The poet clearly implies that he was happy with Cynara, but the relationship is now over. The poet has sought to erase the memory of Cynara by ever-more riotous living and seeking-out of sexual pleasure – but his heart is drawn back to Cynara.

Commentary

This poem is typically world-weary and decadent, and bemoans the loss of true love. It is a poem of lost innocence. Cynara represents the lost love who has now become an obsession. Cynara's pale, lost lilies are contrasted with the bought red mouth of the prostitute that Dowson has spent the night with.

Technically the poem is very interesting. Dowson uses a 12 syllable line (more common in French literature) resorting to an iambic pentameter in the penultimate line of each stanza. This 12 syllable line is called an Alexandrine or hexameter and is very rare in English poetry.

What is its effect? Its length mirrors the languor and ennui that the poet feels and also, it could be argued, prolongs the misery in verse of the misery he feels at his estrangement from Cynara. Furthermore, the fourth and sixth line of each stanza are repeated almost word for word again stressing his obsession with Cynara. Some of Dowson's vocabulary is archaic – *yesternight, betwixt, yea* – and the whole poem is decidedly decadent, but the overall impression is of pure, unfeigned emotion. This is aided by Dowson's use of the caesura. In the poem the strongest caesuras follow Cynara's name – thus highlighting still further his obsession with her.

The first stanza describes the events of the previous night: Dowson has spent it with a prostitute but he cannot rid himself of the memory of Cynara: *betwixt her lips and mine/ There fell thy shadow, Cynara!* And so intense is his memory of Cynara that he writes *thy breath was shed/ Upon my soul between the kisses and the wine.* Dowson makes clear his angst in the fifth line which becomes the refrain of the rest of the poem:

And I was desolate and sick of an old passion.

The second stanza begins with intimate details of the night before:

All night upon mine heart I felt her warm heart beat,

Night-long within mine arms in love and sleep she lay.

Dowson asserts that *the kisses of the prostitute's bought red mouth were sweet,* but Dowson is plunged into despair – partly at the absence of Cynara and partly because he wakes from a night of bought passion to find *the dawn was grey.*

Dowson begins the third stanza by admitting he has forgotten a great deal. Who is the subject of gone with wind? It could be Dowson himself or the things he has forgotten or it could even be Cynara – this is poetry so it could be all three! The next two lines describe the distractions that Dowson has indulged in in an attempt to forget Cynara:

Flung roses, roses riotously with the throng,

Dancing, to put thy pale, lost lilies out of mind.

But this riotous living cannot erase Cynara from his mind:

But I was desolate and sick of an old passion,

>   *Yea, all the time, because the dance was long.*

No distraction, no matter how intense, can ease his passion for Cynara.

In the fourth stanza he calls for *madder music and for stronger wine* in an attempt to forget Cynara and distract himself, but at the end of it all

when the feast is finished and the lamps expire

Then falls thy shadow Cynara! The night is thine.

The last line of each stanza –

I have been faithful to thee, Cynara! in my fashion –

acts as a refrain. The assertion before the caesura sounds confident and strong; by contrast the excuse *in my fashion* (which means having a riotous time with prostitutes) seems rather weak and unconvincing, but at least it is honest. The narrator comes across as a weak and downcast character who cannot resist temptation, despite his stated love for Cynara.

This poem is not typical of the poems in the Anthology. It is typical in that it deals with unrequited love – the poet's yearning for Cynara – but the atmosphere of music, roses and prostitutes, marks it as different in kind. It is different because of the fin de siècle mood and the tired, decadent, world-weary pessimism that runs through the poem and is exemplified by the impossibility of re-establishing a relationship with Cynara. She is *gone with the wind*. Dowson yearns for an unattainable woman from the past and seems powerless to prevent his own decline into despondency, gloom and sadness.

Why?

In this poem Dowson

- paints a compelling and convincing picture of decadence and moral decline;
- makes clear his obsession with a more innocent past, symbolized by Cynara;
- skillfully uses the long Alexandrine line to suggest the agony he is undergoing;
- uses repetition to suggest his continuing obsession with Cynara.

Further reading: *The Poems of Ernest Dowson* ISBN: 978-1511897464

Glossary

The Oxford Concise Dictionary of Literary Terms has been invaluable in writing this section of the book. I would again remind the reader that knowledge of these terms is only the start – do NOT define a word you find here in the examination. You can take it for granted that the examiner knows the term: it is up to you to try to use it confidently and with precision and to explain why the poet uses it or what effect it has on the reader.

ALLITERATION — the repetition of the same sounds – usually initial consonants or stressed syllables – in any sequence of closely adjacent words.

ALLUSION — an indirect or passing reference to some event, person, place or artistic work which is not explained by the writer, but which relies on the reader's familiarity with it.

AMBIGUITY — openness to different interpretations.

ASSONANCE — the repetition of similar vowel sounds in neighbouring words.

BALLAD — a folk song or orally transmitted poem telling in a simple and direct way a story with a tragic ending. Ballads are normally composed in quatrains with the second and fourth lines rhyming. Such quatrains are known as the ballad stanza because of its frequent use in what we call ballads.

BLANK VERSE — unrhymed lines of ten syllable length. This is a widely used form by Shakespeare in his plays, by Milton and by Wordsworth.

CAESURA — any pause in a line of verse caused by punctuation. This can draw attention to what precedes or follows the caesura and also, by breaking up the rhythm of the line, can slow the poem down and make it more like ordinary speech.

CANON

a body of writings recognized by authority. The canon of a national literature is a body of writings especially approved by critics or anthologists and deemed suitable for academic study. Towards the end of the 20th century there was a general feeling that the canon of English Literature was dominated by dead white men and since then there has been a deliberate and fruitful attempt made to give more prominence to writing by women and by writers from non-white backgrounds. Even your Anthology is a contribution to the canon, because someone sat down and decided that the poems included in it were worthy of study by students taking GCSE.

CARPE DIEM

a Latin phrase from the Roman poet Horace which means 'seize the day' – 'make the best of the present moment'. It is a very common theme of European lyric poetry, in which the speaker of a poem argues that since time is short and death is inevitable, pleasure should be enjoyed while there is still time.

COLLOCATION

the act of putting two words together. What this means in practice is that certain words have very common collocations – in other words they are usually found in written or spoken English in collocation with other words. For example, the word *Christmas* is often collocated with words such as *cards*, *presents*, *carols*, *holidays*, but you won't often find it collocated with *sadness*. This can be an important term because poets, who are seeking to use words in original ways, will often put two words together are not often collocated.

COLLOQUIALISM the use of informal expressions or vocabulary appropriate to everyday speech rather than the formality of writing. When used in poetry it can make the poem seem more down-to-earth and real, more honest and intimate.

CONCEIT an unusually far-fetched metaphor presenting a surprising and witty parallel between two apparently dissimilar things or feelings.

CONSONANCE the repetition of identical or similar consonants in neighbouring words whose vowel sounds are different.

CONTEXT the biographical, social, cultural and historical circumstances in which a text is produced and read and understood – you might to think of it as its background. However, it is important sometimes to consider the reader's own context – especially when we look back at poems from the Literary Heritage. To interpret a poem with full regard to its background is to contextualize it.

COUPLET a pair of rhyming verse lines, usually of the same length.

CROSSED RHYME the rhyming of one word in the middle of a long line of poetry with a word in a similar position in the next line.

DIALECT	a distinctive variety of language, spoken by members of an identifiable regional group, nation or social class. Dialects differ from one another in pronunciation, vocabulary and grammar. Traditionally they have been looked down on and viewed as variations from an educated 'standard' form of the language, but linguists point out that standard forms themselves are merely dialects which have come to dominate for social and political reasons. In English this notion of dialect is especially important because English is spoken all over the world and there are variations between the English spoken in, say, Yorkshire, Delhi and Australia. Dialects now are increasingly celebrated as a distinct way of speaking and writing which are integral to our identity.
DICTION	the choice of words used in any literary work.
DISSONANCE	harshness of sound.
DRAMATIC MONOLOGUE	a kind of poem in which a single fictional or historical character (not the poet) speaks to a silent audience and unwittingly reveals the truth about their character.
ELEGY	a lyric poem lamenting the death of a friend or public figure or reflecting seriously on a serious subject. The elegiac has come to refer to the mournful mood of such poems.

ELLIPSIS	the omission from a sentence of a word or words which would be required for complete clarity. It is used all the time in everyday speech, but is often used in poetry to promote compression and/or ambiguity. The adjective is elliptical.
END-RHYME	rhyme occurring at the end of a line of poetry. The most common form of rhyme.
END-STOPPED	a line of poetry brought to a pause by the use of punctuation. The opposite of enjambment.
ENJAMBMENT	caused by the lack of punctuation at the end of a line of poetry, this causes the sense (and the voice when the poem is read aloud) to 'run over' into the next line. In general, this can impart to poems the feel of ordinary speech, but there are examples in the Anthology of more precise reasons for the poet to use enjambment.
EPIPHANY usually	a sudden moment of insight or revelation, at the end of a poem.
EPIZEUXIS or ZEUXIS	the technique by which a word is repeated for emphasis with no other words intervening
EUPHONY	a pleasing smoothness of sound
FIGURATIVE	Not literal. Obviously 'figurative' language covers metaphor and simile and personification
FIGURE OF SPEECH	any expression which departs from the ordinary literal sense or normal order of words. Figurative language

(the opposite of literal language) includes metaphor, simile and personification. Some figures of speech – such as alliteration and assonance achieve their effects through the repetition of sounds.

FOREGROUNDING   giving unusual prominence to one part of a text. Poetry differs from everyday speech and prose by its use of regular rhythm, metaphors, alliteration and other devices by which its language draws attention to itself.

FREE VERSE   a kind of poetry that does not conform to any regular pattern of line length or rhyme. The length of its lines are irregular as its use of rhyme – if any.

HALF-RHYME   an imperfect rhyme – also known as para-rhyme, near rhyme and slant rhyme – in which the final consonants but the vowel sounds do not match or where the vowels match but the consonants differ. Pioneered in the 19th century by the Emily Dickinson and Gerard Manley Hopkins, and made even more popular by Wilfred Owen and T S Eliot in the early 20th century, the use of half-rhyme is often an indication that the poet wants to suggest a feeling of unease and disquiet.

HOMONYM   a word that is identical to another word either in sound or in spelling

HOMOPHONE   a word that is pronounced in the same way as another word but which differs in meaning and/or spelling.

HYPERBOLE   exaggeration for the sake of emphasis.

IDIOM   an everyday phrase that cannot be translated literally because its meaning does not correspond to the specific words in the phrase. There are thousands in English like – *you get up my nose, when pigs fly, she was all ears.*

IMAGERY   a rather vague critical term covering literal and metaphorical language which evoke sense impressions with reference to concrete objects – the things the writer describes.

INTERNAL RHYME   a poetic device in which two or more words in the same line rhyme.

INTERTEXTUALITY   the relationship that a text may have with anoth preceding and usually well-known text.

INVERSION   the reversal of the normally expected order or words. 'Normally expected' means how we might say the words in the order of normal speech; to invert the normal word order usually draws attention or foregrounds the words.

JUXTAPOSITION two things that are placed alongside each other.

LAMENT   any poem expressing profound grief usually in the face of death.

LATINATE   Latinate diction in English means the use of words derived from Latin rather than those derived from Old English.

LITOTES	understatement – the opposite of hyperbole.
LYRIC	any fairly short poem expressing the personal mood of the speaker.
METAPHOR	the most important figure of speech in which in which one thing is referred to by a word normally associated with another thing, so as to suggest some common quality shared by both things. In metaphor, this similarity is directly stated, unlike in a simile where the resemblance is indirect and introduced by the words like or as. Much of our everyday language is made up of metaphor too – to say someone is as greedy as a pig is a simile; to say he is a pig is a metaphor.
MNEMONIC	a form of words or letters that helps people remember things. It is common in everyday sayings and uses some of the features of language that we associate with poetry. For example, the weather saying Red sky at night, shepherd's delight uses rhyme.
MONOLOGUE`	an extended speech uttered by one speaker.
NARRATOR of the poem.	the one who tells or is assumed to be the voice

OCTAVE or OCTET a group of eight lines forming the first part of a sonnet.

ONOMATOPOEIA	the use of words that seem to imitate the sounds they refer to (*bang, whizz, crackle, fizz*) or any combination or words in which the sound echoes or seems to echo the sense. The adjective is onomatopoeic, so you can say that *blast* is an onomatopoeic word.

ORAL TRADITION the passing on from one generation to another of songs, chants, poems, proverbs by word of mouth and memory.

OXYMORON a figure of speech that combines two seemingly contradictory terms as in the everyday terms bitter-sweet and living death.

PARALLELISM the arrangement of similarly constructed clause, sentences or lines of poetry.

PARADOX a statement which is self-contradictory.

PATHETIC FALLACY this is the convention that natural phenomena (usually the weather) are a reflection of the poet's or the narrator's mood. It may well involve the personification of things in nature, but does not have to. At its simplest, a writer might choose to associate very bad weather with a mood of depression and sadness.

PERSONA the assumed identity or fictional narrator assumed by a writer.

PERSONIFICATION a figure of speech in which animals, abstract ideas or lifeless things are referred to as if they were human. Sometimes known as personal metaphor.

PETRARCHAN characteristic of the Italian poet Petrarch (1304 – 1374). Mainly applied to the Petrarchan sonnet which is different in its form from the Shakespearean sonnet.

PHONETIC SPELLING a technique writers use which involves misspelling a word in order to imitate the accent in which the word is said.

PLOSIVE

explosive. Used to describe sounds that we form by putting our lips together such as *b* and *p*.

POSTCOLONIAL LITERATURE

a term devised to describe what used to be called Commonwealth Literature (and before that Empire Writing!). The term covers a very wide range of writing from countries that were once colonies of European countries. It has come to include some writing by writers of non-white racial backgrounds whose roots or family originated in former colonies – no matter where they live now.

PUN

an expression that derives humour either through using a word that has two distinct meanings or two similar sounding words (homophones).

QUATRAIN

a verse stanza of four lines – usually rhymed.

REFRAIN

a line, or a group of lines, repeated at intervals throughout a poem – usually at regular intervals and at the end of a stanza.

RHYME

the identity of sound between syllables or paired groups of syllables usually at the end of a line of poetry.

RHYME SCHEME   the pattern in which the rhymed line endings are arranged in any poem or stanza. This is normally written as a sequence of letters where each line ending in the same rhyme is given the same alphabetical letter. So a Shakespearean sonnet's rhyme scheme is ababcdcdefefgg, but the rhyme scheme of a Petrarchan sonnet is abbaabbacdecde. In other poems the rhyme scheme might be arranged to suit the poet's convenience or intentions. For example, in Blake's 'London' the first stanza rhymes abab, the second cdcd and so on.

RHYTHM   a pattern of sounds which is repeated with the stress falling on the same syllables (more or less) in each line. However, variations to the pattern, especially towards the end of the poem, often stand out and are foregrounded because they break the pattern the poet has built up through the course of the poem.

ROMANTICISM   the name given to the artistic movement that emerged in England and Germany in the 19790a and in the rest of Europe in the 1820s and beyond. It was a movement that saw great changes in literature, painting, sculpture, architecture and music and found its catalyst in the new philosophical ideas of Jean Jacques Rousseau and Thomas Paine, and in response to the French and industrial revolutions. Its chief emphasis was on freedom of individual self-expression, sincerity, spontaneity and originality, but it also looked to the distant past of the Middle Ages for some of its inspiration.

SATIRE   any type of writing which exposes and mocks

the foolishness or evil of individuals, institutions or societies. A poem can be satiric (adjective) or you can say a poet satirizes something or somebody.

SESTET	a group of six lines forming the second half of a sonnet, following the octet.
SIBILANCE	the noticeable recurrence of *s* sounds.
SIMILE	an explicit comparison between two different things, actions or feelings, usually introduced by *like* or *as*.
SONNET	a lyric poem of 14 lines of equal length. The form originated in Italy and was made famous as a vehicle for love poetry by Petrarch and came to be adopted throughout Europe. The standard subject matter of early sonnets was romantic love, but in the 17th century John Donne used it to write religious poetry and John Milton wrote political sonnets, so it came to be used for any subject matter. The sonnet form enjoyed a revival in the Romantic period (Wordsworth, Keats and Shelley all wrote them) and continues to be widely used today. Some poets have written connected series of sonnets and these are known as sonnet cycles. Petrarchan sonnets differ slightly in their rhyme scheme from Shakespearean sonnets (see the entry above on rhyme scheme). A Petrarchan sonnet consists of two quatrains (the octet) followed by two tercets (the sestet). A Shakespearean sonnet consist of two quatrains (the octet) followed by another quatrain and a final couplet (the sestet).
STANZA	a group of verse lines forming a section of a

poem and sharing the same structure in terms of the length of the lines, the rhyme scheme and the rhythm.

STYLE
any specific way of using language, which is characteristic of an author, a period, a type of poetry or a group of writers.

SYLLOGISM
a form of logical argument that draws a conclusion from two propositions. It is very characteristic of Metaphysical poetry and is exemplified in the anthology by Marvell's 'To His Coy Mistress'.

SYMBOL
anything that represents something else. A national flag symbolizes the country that uses it; symbols are heavily used in road signs. In poetry symbols can represent almost anything. Blake's 'The Sick Rose' and Armitage's 'Harmonium' are two good examples of symbols dealt with in this book.

SYNECDOCHE
a figure of speech in which a thing or person is referred to indirectly, either by naming some part of it (*hands* for manual labourers) or by naming some big thing of which it is a part (the law for police officers). As you can see from these examples, it is a common practice in speech.

TONE
a critical term meaning the mood or atmosphere of a piece of writing. It may also include the sense of the writer's attitude to the reader of the subject matter.

TURN
the English term for a sudden change in mood or line of argument, especially in line 9 of a sonnet.

VERSE

another word for poetry as opposed to prose. The use of the word 'verse' sometimes implies writing that rhymes and has a rhythm, but perhaps lacks the merit of real poetry.

VERSE PARAGRAPH

a group of lines of poetry forming a section of a poem, the length of the unit being determined by the sense rather than a particular stanza pattern. Marvell's 'To His Coy Mistress' consists of verse paragraphs.

VOLTA

the Italian term for the 'turn' in the argument or mood of a sonnet which normally occurs in the ninth line at the start of the sestet, but sometimes in Shakespearean sonnets is delayed until the final couplet.

WIT

a general term which covers the idea of intelligence, but refers in poetry more specifically to verbal ingenuity and cleverness or bizarre and unexpected comparisons.

CPSIA information can be obtained
at www.ICGtesting.com
Printed in the USA
LVHW021737210119
604669LV00017B/1334/P

9 781911 477068